OTHER BOOKS BY JANE E. VENNARD

Praying for Friends and Enemies

*Praying for Body and Soul:
A Way to Intimacy with God*

*Be Still:
Designing and Leading Contemplative Retreats*

Embracing
the World

Embracing the World

Praying for Justice and Peace

JANE E. VENNARD

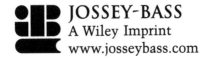

JOSSEY-BASS
A Wiley Imprint
www.josseybass.com

Published by Jossey-Bass
A Wiley Imprint
989 Market Street, San Francisco, CA 94103-1741   www.josseybass.com

Jossey-Bass books and products are available through most bookstores. To contact Jossey-Bass directly call our Customer Care Department within the U.S. at 800-956-7739, outside the U.S. at 317-572-3986 or fax 317-572-4002.

Jossey-Bass also publishes its books in a variety of electronic formats. Some content that appears in print may not be available in electronic books.

Credits are on page 147.

Library of Congress Cataloging-in-Publication Data
Vennard, Jane E. (Jane Elizabeth), date
    Embracing the world: praying for justice and peace/Jane E. Vennard. 1st ed.
        p. cm.
Includes bibliographical references and index.
    ISBN 0-7879-5887-5 (alk. paper)
    1. Prayer—Christianity. 2. Christianity and justice. 3. Peace—Religious aspects—Christianity. I. Title.
BV210.3.V46 2002
248.3'2—dc21   2002012720

Printed in the United States of America
FIRST EDITION
HB Printing   10 9 8 7 6 5 4 3 2 1

CONTENTS

For my stepsons
Jamie and Paul Laurie

In the spring of 1999, Professor Dana Wilbanks, chair of Justice and Peace Studies at the Iliff School of Theology in Denver where I am senior adjunct faculty in prayer and spirituality, asked me if I would teach a course connecting spirituality with the work of justice and peace. We talked for a while, shared some ideas, and came up with "Praying for Justice and Peace" as the title for the class. "We'll schedule it for next spring," Dana said as he left. "Thanks a lot."

I was excited about the prospect of designing and teaching a new course, but I soon found myself overcome with fear and a sense of inadequacy. My first doubt came in very specific form. I asked myself, "How can I teach about justice and peace when I never march?" This may seem like an odd question, but I have always associated people who were justice and peace activists with those who went to freedom marches, peace demonstrations, and actions for the rights of the marginalized. On reflection, I realized that this feeling of inadequacy was connected to my long-time guilt that I had not been involved in the civil rights movement. During the early 1960s, I was living overseas. When I returned home, my mind and heart were turned to other things. I was involved in marriage and career, and in striving for upward mobility. As I anticipated teaching about justice and peace, I became aware that I had not forgiven myself for my lack of awareness and my inaction at a critical period of our nation's history. Maybe teaching this class would allow me to let go of that old pain.

As I wrestled with those issues, another question arose. "How can I teach about justice and peace when I have never been on mission?" I have never served in Africa, Asia, or Central America and have never visited the Middle East. I have not done ministry in rural America or our inner cities, or even spent a Thanksgiving in a food line serving the homeless and the hungry. I have never experienced the physical hardships of poverty, hunger, homelessness, or war. I realized I was embarrassed by my middle-class life.

Wrestling with my own inadequacies, I remembered the words of a wise spiritual director. "You have many advantages," he told me. "You are white, educated, economically comfortable. The question is not, Why do you have these gifts and graces? but rather, How can you use them to serve God?" His compassionate response helped me to reflect on how, in my own unique life, I have served God by praying and acting for justice and peace. After my former husband realized at age thirty-two that he was gay, I began to teach others about the issues surrounding sexual orientation and to work for full inclusion of gay, lesbian, and bisexual people in society and in congregations. In seminary, I was involved in the Center for Women and Religion, which not only advocated for women's rights but helped to heal deep wounds caused by the oppression and exclusion of women throughout the history of Christianity. In my personal life, I have tried to serve as a peacemaker, helping family and friends resolve conflicts and find reconciliation with those from whom they were estranged. "Bloom where you are planted," someone once said. Maybe that was what I had been doing in my work for justice and peace.

As I pondered and prayed about my own experiences, I began to realize that there were other people who felt as I did—people who were not on the public front lines but who cared deeply about justice and peace and were acting and speaking in small and quiet ways: parents teaching their children how to solve conflicts without violence, young adults speaking out against prejudice at their own family gatherings, teenagers drawing close to protect a young boy from bullying, teachers telling the hard stories from the underside of history, librarians and booksellers standing firm against censorship, retired folk showing up faithfully in a neighborhood school's reading program, and the homebound stuffing envelopes soliciting funds for the city's homeless shelter. Maybe all these people were activists, blooming where they were planted, quietly doing the work of justice and peace.

When I shared these ideas about quiet activism with a small group, they were relieved; many had the same doubts that I had. "I really have thought of myself simply as a stay-at-home mom," one woman told the group. "Certainly not an activist. But as we are talking, I realize that earlier this year I went to my son's kindergarten teacher and told her that the way she was treating some of the children was not right. That was an action for justice in my own back yard."

A retired engineer said, "Just last week I was with a group of guys helping clean up the neighborhood school yard. One of the men told a sexist joke, and everyone laughed but me. I took a deep breath and said that I did not find jokes that demeaned others funny. Everyone was silent and then we went back to work."

"I am spending a lot of time trying to bring reconciliation between my mother and my sister," a woman added. "I never thought I was involved in peace work, but I guess I am."

"Well, I am a not-so-quiet-activist,"[1] an energized young woman practically shouted. "I'm angry at injustice, and my anger motivates me to act in a public way. I march, I demonstrate, and I imagine someday I will be arrested for my convictions. Quiet activism is fine, but people are also needed on the front lines. Let's be sure we affirm all kinds of actions for justice and peace."

The people in that group and others like them around the world are those Sala Nolan of the United Church of Christ National Office of Witness and Peace Ministries calls the soldiers of the movement. "We cannot all be Gandhi or Martin Luther King Jr. We cannot all be leaders," she told me. "But it is just as important to be followers. Many are those who listen and answer the call in a variety of ways. They are everywhere, all over the planet. They need to know how important they are and how the work of justice and peace depends on their prayers, their words, and their actions."

The people's stories plus Sala's wisdom reassured me that my unwillingness to march and my lack of mission experience did not disqualify me from teaching a class on justice and peace and, ultimately, from writing this book. But then came the next question: How does one actually pray for justice and peace? In my writing and teaching about prayer, I have always stressed that prayer does not take us out of the world but draws us more fully into the world. I have pointed to the connection between contemplation and action, seeing them not as opposites but as integrally connected. I speak about a prayer and action cycle where prayer leads us into service and service leads us to reflection and back to God. In prayer, we gather strength and courage to return to a hurting world that only reminds us of our dependence on God to do God's work of love and compassion. But now I needed to do more than acknowledge the connection between prayer and action. I was being challenged to articulate specific methods of praying for justice and peace.

In my thinking and planning, I decided to begin with the most common and therefore the most familiar way to pray for justice and peace: *intercessory prayer.* In this form of prayer, we ask God to intercede in places of war and oppression so that peace may be made and justice done. We ask God to guide, encourage, and protect those people who are working for peace and justice around the world and in our own communities and families. We offer prayers of intercession not only as individuals but as communities of faith, where intercessory prayers are a part of corporate worship and are regularly included in liturgy.

Prayers of intercession are usually offered in verbal form and addressed to God. Because I know that praying with words is not the only way to pray, I recognized another method of praying for justice and peace, and I called these *action prayers.* Action prayers are when we speak or act in any way for the sake of justice and peace. With our attention on God and our intention to do God's work in the world, actions can become prayer. Writing a letter to a congressperson, teaching conflict resolution skills, going to a forum on interfaith dialogue, and demonstrating at the School of the Americas are actions that can become prayer. We are praying with our bodies—our voices, our hands, our feet.

Praying and acting for justice and peace opens our eyes to the many needs in the world. We may see so many opportunities for service that we are often in danger of succumbing to overwork and wearing ourselves out. Before this happens, we are in need of *prayers of renewal.* Prayers of renewal guide us into a deeper relationship with God so that we remember in whose name we act and reconnect to the love and compassion needed to sustain our actions for justice and peace. Making music, walking, swimming, reading, painting, gardening, journaling, writing poetry, and finding silence are some of the ways that people pray to be renewed and revitalized. Our deep connection with God brings us courage, strength, and enthusiasm for the role we are to play in creating the kingdom of God.

When we pray for justice and peace in any of these three ways, we open ourselves to the possibility of transformation. Our intention to be with God and to do God's work in the world opens us to God's grace so that our prayers, our hearts, and our very lives may be transformed. To open more fully to this transformative power, we can examine our own hearts for seeds of violence, prejudice, hate, and revenge, and we can pray for healing. We might also learn to be silent and still before God, simply placing ourselves in God's presence, allowing ourselves to be changed in ways we cannot imagine. When we turn inward to examine our hearts and then silently wait, we are engaged in *prayers of transformation* that invite God to do the work of justice and peace in our own hearts.

After I had recognized these four ways of praying for justice and peace, I numbered them, believing that intercession would be first, action second, renewal third, and transformation fourth. As I put them out in linear form, I realized instantly that they should be in a circle, for the process of prayer does not have as its goal personal transformation; rather, the process of prayer leads us more deeply into relationship with God and more fully into the world. So of course the prayers of transformation would open our hearts and lead us back into praying for others, into new action, and to the need for renewal. After I had articulated these four ways to pray for justice and peace and had created a circular structure to contain them, I realized I had a model from which I could teach. I was pleased and ready to present my ideas.

The first time I presented the model and explained the four ways of praying, a woman responded thoughtfully. "I would remove the numbers," she said. "I don't think everyone starts with intercessory prayer. I know I began by acting for justice and peace, and from there I was led to prayers for renewal." A man chimed in. "I think the arrows need to go in both directions," he said. "I began with intercessory prayer. Those prayers were transformative, and I felt called to go more deeply into meditation and silent prayer." Another participant added, "The arrows need to go across the circle as well. Couldn't someone be engaged in transformative prayer and move directly into action?" As we shared experiences and played with connections, the model that emerged looked like the illustration below.

Many months later, after I had presented the material to another group, a man came to me after our closing prayer and said, "I think there is something missing. You imply the need for discernment in all four ways of praying. But praying for discernment is an important part of praying for justice and peace. I think you need to add discernment as a fifth way to pray."

I thanked him for his suggestion, but I was not sure I wanted to hear it. When I was in the process of formulating my ideas, I welcomed questions and new ideas. But once I had my model, I didn't want to change it. I was too tired to wrestle with the problem at the moment, but his words had a strong impact on me. It wasn't many weeks before I knew

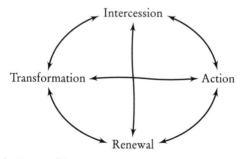

A Circular Process of Prayer.

he was right. Discernment needed to be specifically explored as a fifth way of praying for justice and peace. Praying for discernment is opening ourselves to God's will and promise for us and the world. These prayers guide us in choosing our actions and the ways we need to pray. They remind us that we are working for God's justice and peace and not for our own. Discernment is truly at the heart of the matter. In gratitude for his insight, I added discernment to the model. It now looks like the illustration below.

I have presented the model and explored the five ways we pray for justice and peace with a variety of people in a number of settings. They have enriched and strengthened my original ideas with new insights, experiences of prayer, and wonderful stories of action. The book that has emerged from these interactive experiences is far more than I ever dreamed it could be as I planned a class three years ago and later designed this book around the five ways to pray for justice and peace. Each chapter of *Embracing the World* explores in detail one form of prayer through description, explanation, and stories, as well as biblical and theological reflections. The chapters end with an invitation to pray that will guide you into a prayer experience and encourage you

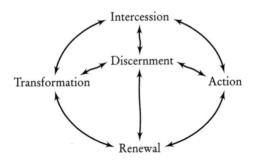

A Circular Process with Discernment at the Center.

to practice praying for justice and peace. Because a book is in linear form and chapters need to be numbered, I have placed the five ways of praying in their original sequence. However, they need not be read in that order. Feel free to start reading anywhere, knowing that each prayer form is connected to another and to the whole. Wherever you begin, you will be led to the next step on your own prayer journey.

The five chapters on the forms of prayer are bracketed with an opening and a closing chapter. The first chapter grounds us in God, who initiates all prayer and whose peace and justice we strive to make a reality. I share my assumptions about prayer, including the premise that prayer is our primary action in a world faced with injustice, oppression, and war. I explore the deep meaning of *shalom* to discover that peace is not just the absence of war but a living, vibrant entity in itself. I offer a description of justice that takes us beyond fairness to embrace the experience of mercy as an integral part of God's promise and hope for our world.

The last chapter explores the experience of mercy more fully and examines how we are dependent on the mercy of God when praying for justice and peace. Thomas Merton, a Trappist monk and peace activist, understood God to be "Mercy with Mercy within Mercy."[2] I explore this theology and present ways we can pay attention to God's mercy in our own lives and in the life of the world. I close with my understanding of how trusting the mercy of God leads us from despair to hope and how hope is what keeps us praying for justice and peace and keeps us faithful to God's vision of a new heaven and a new earth.

I write this book from a Christian perspective, for that is my tradition. However, I draw from the wisdom of many faith traditions and believe deeply that all prayers for justice and peace transcend tradition, language, and culture and are heard by the same loving and merciful God. People of all faiths are called to cooperate in the struggle to create a loving and peaceful world in partnership with God and one another. We are in this holy work together.

Embracing the World is for everyone who cares about making the world a better place and who longs to live in harmony with all creation. You may be a professional activist, a front-line activist, or a quiet activist. Or you may not think of yourself as an activist at all. You may be a person of deep and faithful prayer who knows without a doubt that prayer makes a difference; you may be new to prayer, questioning the efficacy of prayer. Or you may think of yourself as someone who does not pray. However you identify yourself through action or prayer, this book is written for you. As you read, my hope is that you will discover the power of prayer in bringing about justice and peace and the power you have in your own life to participate in the reign of God. God calls all of us. God depends on all of us. God believes in all of us. Together we can be about God's work, co-creating a world of justice and peace.

Praying for justice and peace is a prophetic act that calls us to stretch our arms out wide and embrace the whole world. In holy boldness we cover the earth with the grace and the mercy of God.

—RICHARD FOSTER

Embracing
the World

CHAPTER ONE

GROUNDING OURSELVES IN GOD

Rooted in God we rise up in justice.

—EDWINA GATELEY

When I ask participants on retreat how they learned to pray, I am usually greeted with a stunned silence. Then someone will say, "Wow, that was a long time ago." Another might add, "I've never asked myself that question." As they begin to reflect and remember, they share a range of experiences.

"My mother taught me the words to the prayers of our Catholic tradition and listened to me recite them every night," one woman might say.

"I learned those too," a man interjects, "but my father who was a long-distance trucker taught me to just talk to God with my own words and feelings."

"No one taught me to pray," a young woman adds thoughtfully. "But I knew my grandmother prayed. I was curious, but never asked her about it."

"I learned to pray in Sunday School where I went with my best friend," a retired schoolteacher tells the group. "I couldn't pray at home because my family was scornful of religion and prayer."

"What seems odd to me," an older man says shyly, "is that no one taught me to pray, but I have been praying as long as I can remember. Maybe God taught me to pray."

How did you learn to pray? Those early experiences of prayer are important in praying for justice and peace because they are the basis for how we pray. They also hold at their center our assumptions about prayer and about God—who God is in our lives and how we are present to God through prayer. We have to be aware of what those assumptions are in order to begin our exploration of what it means to pray for justice and peace or we may get stuck in those early lessons. Whether you still pray the way you were taught, have discovered other ways to pray, or have even stopped praying altogether, understanding these core assumptions from childhood is essential to opening to the possibilities of praying for peace and justice.

As you read this chapter, consider taking time to reflect on the assumptions you grew up with, whether you still accept them or disagree with them now. How do those assumptions influence how you pray and your willingness to learn new ways to pray and grow in your relationship with God?

What Is Prayer?

Prayer is relational. Prayer is about growing closer to God and deepening our relationship with God. When we first learn to pray, we are being introduced to God. As we pursue prayer, we become more friendly with God. In time, that friendship may blossom and offer the possibility of intimacy, just as a human friendship may grow in intimacy over time and with more intentional contact. We might think of our relationship with God as similar to an intimate human relationship in which two people merge with one another, even as they remain separate. They become so close that they may know each other's thoughts, dream the same dreams, and sense when the other is in need. And yet, even in that closeness, each one can find room to grow, space to explore, and the ability to surprise the other. It is possible to grow into this kind of intimate relationship with God, as some of the great mystics and saints have done.

One of my favorite stories is about St. Teresa of Avila, a sixteenth-century mystic who felt so close to God that she was willing to express all her thoughts and feelings in her intimate relationship. One dark night, she was traveling through northern Spain to the site of a new monastery. A fierce storm came upon her and her traveling companions. The wheels of the wagon got stuck in the mud, halting all progress. Teresa climbed down from her perch into the pouring rain, raised her face and her fist to God and shouted, "If this is the way you treat your friends, no wonder you have so few!"

You may not think of yourself as a mystic, but you may long for a deeper relationship with God, just as God wants greater intimacy with you. God's desire for that intimacy with us is sometimes hard to believe. We may feel unworthy, unwilling to respond or even question the existence of God. But God knows us all, loves us all, and wants closeness with us. As the Lord told Jeremiah, "Before I formed you in the womb I knew you, and before you were born I consecrated you" (Jeremiah 1:5). How can we believe and trust that God yearns for us just as we yearn for God?

God's longing for us sometimes makes us want to pray. So when people tell me they long to pray but they do not know how or have forgotten, I tell them that their wanting and their longing *is* prayer. In that longing, they feel God's call in the stirring of their hearts, and they want to respond. When we feel like praying or begin to pray in any form, we are responding to God's invitation to closeness. We are simply saying yes!

Any yes to God that honors and strengthens and deepens our relationship with God is prayer. Anything and everything can become a prayer, but nothing is automatically a prayer. Prayer requires both intention and attention. The way we approach an activity signals what we intend, what it means. If I seek to find God in my walk through the woods, my walk becomes a prayer. If I open myself to God's presence in a conversation with a friend, our discussion becomes a prayer. If I ask for God's guidance when I enter a difficult meeting, the meeting becomes a prayer. Yet if I walk to get my heart rate up, or spend time with my friend because I like her, or go to meetings to get things done, these activities—healthy, enjoyable, and productive though they may be—are not prayer. When I remember my intention to pray or when God grabs my attention in the midst of an activity, my action becomes a prayer.

When God grabs my attention, I become present to God with mind and heart and body, and I turn my action into prayer. Attention will allow me to see God in the smile of a child, in the embrace of my friend, even in the eyes of an adversary. When we are open to God's presence, we discover God is always with us. God calls us to intention and attention. God calls us into prayer.

God also reminds us that prayer is an embodied activity, not an ethereal abstraction. God came to us in human form. Jesus, born of a woman, suckled and cried, worked and played, grew into manhood, ate and drank, laughed and wept. He touched and healed and shared his anger. He cried out in fear. He died a physical death. And all the time he was in deep intimacy with his Abba, his Father. God wants all of our humanness, including our bodies, in relationship.

God even wants all of our emotions to be included in the relationship, not just our awe and our confession and our praise. God wants our anger and our fear, our doubts and our confusion, our passion and our sexuality. God wants our joy and our laughter and our tears. We are called to bring all of who we are into relationship with God. Honoring the gift of our full humanity allows us to pray with movement as well as with stillness, with silence as well as with speech, with music and images as well as with words. Fully embodied prayer excludes nothing.

Our rich, full, passionate prayers are heard by God. They do not fall on deaf ears or a hardened heart. Our longings and desires, our doubts and fears, our hopes and celebrations—all that is in our hearts is welcomed into the heart of God. And how does God respond? Sometimes with answers, sometimes with a challenge, sometimes with comfort, and sometimes with silence.

When God responds with comfort, we feel God's presence in the midst of our struggles and our pain. We know that God cries out with us in our anger, weeps with us in our grief, and holds us in our despair. When God responds to our prayers with a challenge, we may be startled out of our complacency and pointed in a new direction. Occasionally, God answers our prayers clearly and immediately. More often, our prayers are answered with subtle signs, through unlikely messengers, and in God's time rather than our own.

Our all-too-human temptation when we hear silence in response to our prayers is to believe that God does not hear us, that God is absent, or that God is punishing us with silence. But think of a friend who listens to you with her heart. She hears you so completely she need say nothing. Her listening presence is gift enough. Could it be that God's listening is sometimes all we need? If so, God's silence becomes a gift.

Praying in the World

Some people think of prayer as an escape from the world. I once heard a man of deep prayer described as "someone who was so heavenly he was no earthly good."

But divisions between heaven and earth, spirit and matter, and contemplation and action are artificial. As peace activist Dorothy Friesen said, "People have often been suspicious of prayer as belonging to the realm of those pious ones who hide behind words to avoid involvement. But the split between people of prayer and people of action is a false and harmful one."[1]

Once during a class, I invited the students to place themselves on a scale of one to ten, where one was the designation for a contemplative (a person of prayer) and ten was the designation for an activist (a person of action). They could use any number between one and ten to describe themselves. Some seemed to know immediately where they belonged, and others struggled to place themselves on the scale and then to explain their decision to each other.

One student remembered how active she had been in college, attending rallies and marches and going to the state capitol to lobby for legislation. Now she was a wife, a mother of twins, and a full-time graduate student. She had time for little else. She was not sure where she belonged on the scale. Another student said that he was active in the work of reconciliation, helping individuals and groups who were in conflict. He spent much time in prayer preparing himself for meetings that were often difficult and stressful. He wondered whether this calling made him more of a contemplative or an activist.

As the students listened to one another, they realized that any fixed placement was inaccurate and that contemplatives and activists were not polar opposites. They decided that the line should become a circle in which 1 and 10 are not opposite but united, making contemplation and action inseparable.

Maintaining a separation between contemplation and action wastes our energy in argument and self-righteous posturing. Rather than try to convince ourselves or others that prayer is more effective than direct action or that action in the face of injustice is superior to prayer, we can understand the two to be of equal importance. Then we can use our energy to join with others and with God to bring a world of justice and peace into reality. Through uniting prayer and action, we are able to love and serve the world. In the words of Meister Eckhart, fourteenth-century mystic, "What we have gathered in contemplation we give out in love."[2]

Even when we know that contemplation and action are one, we sometimes forget the importance of prayer in the heat of an activity. I once heard a story of a church committee struggling with an issue that was dividing the congregation. During a meeting where the discussion was going nowhere and tempers were rising, one member suggested they postpone the discussion until the next meeting and in the intervening weeks pray about the issue and pray for resolution and reconciliation. Another committee member pushed back his chair in disgust and said, "Good heavens! Have we come to *that*?" This story, though humorous, points to the false assumption that prayer is a last resort rather than primary and radical action.

And nowhere is this primacy of prayer more true than when it is on behalf of justice and peace. Karl Barth, twentieth-century German theologian, wrote, "To clasp our hands in prayer is the beginning of an uprising against the disorders of the world."[3] Praying for justice and peace forces us to face the disorders of the world and ask ourselves what we can do. Drawing on all our assumptions about who God is and how we can be present to God through prayer, we turn to God for guidance. God can help us envision a world where justice is the norm and people live in peace. God can give us courage to pursue the vision, clarity about the path we are to take toward the vision, and strength to continue when we experience obstacles, setbacks, and dead ends. But before we explore the ways we pray and work for justice and peace, we need to have a clear picture of what we are praying for. What does a just and peaceful world look like? Is everyone treated exactly the same? Is peace defined by the absence of war? What are we trying to bring into reality when we pray for justice and peace?

Fairness, Justice, and Mercy

It's common for children to scream at each other when they feel they have not been treated fairly. "She got more than me! It's not fair!" a little girl may yell about her sister's portion of ice cream. "How come I have to do the dishes and not him," a boy may grumble about his older brother. "It's not fair!" If we are honest, these same sentiments linger into adulthood, even if we do not say them out loud. "It's not fair," you think when your colleague is promoted and you are not. "It's not fair," you sigh when your poem is rejected by a magazine. "It's not fair," you complain when your car is broken into and your neighbor's is left untouched.

The concept of fairness is based on the belief that everything should be equal. But as many have pointed out so often, life is not fair. Children know this, even as they rail against unfairness. Yet fairness does need to be considered in our search for justice because what is known as procedural justice "is concerned with 'fair play,' with ensuring that . . . laws and legal processes are the same for everybody, and are enforced the same for everybody."[4] Equality in procedural justice is important, but it does not address the issues of social justice. As biblical scholar Marcus Borg goes on to say,

Social justice is concerned with the structures of society and their results. Do they produce a large impoverished class or result in a more equitable distribution of resources? Do they produce conflict or peace? Do they destroy or nourish a future? Social justice is concerned with the justice of social systems.[5]

While I was in seminary, I took a class titled "The Parables of Jesus." After a wonderful ten weeks of study, the professor asked us to choose the parable we liked the *least* for our final paper. "The one you would rather skip over, the one that rubs you the wrong way, the one you don't understand, the one you hate," he told us. I chose the Laborers in the Vineyard, which is found in Matthew 20:1–16.

In this parable, a landowner hired laborers for his vineyard. He sent a group in at the earliest hour, another group at nine o'clock, another at noon, and finally a group at five o'clock. When evening came, the landowner instructed his manager to pay the laborers, beginning with those who began work at five. Much to their amazement, they received the full daily wage. Those who had worked longer expected to receive more, but they too received the same. They grumbled against the landowner saying, "These last worked only one hour, and you have made them equal to us who have borne the burden of the day and the scorching heat" (20:12). I sympathized with those laborers who had worked all day. I would have grumbled, too, because it wasn't fair.

As I pondered the story, I found that even more than the unfairness, I was disturbed by the intimation that Jesus was describing God's way of behaving toward humans. Jesus began the parable with the words, "For the kingdom of heaven is like a landowner" (20:1). I didn't like to think of a God who was unfair, but I remembered years ago when I was teaching elementary school that I used to say to my students when they accused me of unfair treatment, "I am not treating you all the same, because you are not all the same. You are different. I am treating you differently according to your needs. That may not seem fair, but it is just."

As I continued to wrestle with the story, I began to see that if God was not fair, at least God was just. With a wider view than mine or the views of the laborers, God transcended the rules of fairness. God understood the desperate need of all the workers for money, no matter when they began work; therefore, the landowner generously paid everyone the daily wage. Upon this reflection, I felt a little better about God, who, although not fair, was just and generous. I wrote an acceptable paper, but the parable still rankled, still disturbed, and remained my least favorite of them all.

Years later, I attended a conference with Father Thomas Keating, a Benedictine monk who writes and teaches about centering prayer. In the midst of his talk, Father Keating referred to this same parable and said very simply that the story was not about a just and generous God. It was a story about a merciful God, a God who pours out God's love on those who work and those who don't work, on those who are sinful and those who are righteous, on those who deserve and those who do not deserve. At once, the words of Shakespeare from *The Merchant of Venice,* which I had memorized in high school, came back to me: "The quality of mercy is not strained, it droppeth as the gentle rain from heaven upon the place beneath. It is twice blest; it blesseth him that gives and him that takes."[6] A merciful God. How could I have missed it? I had focused on the issue of fairness and had given that up for the idea of being treated justly and generously. But the possibility of being treated mercifully filled me with wonder.

This matter of fairness, justice, and mercy struck me again when I read Gerald Sittser's article[7] in *The Christian Century* about losing his mother, wife, and daughter in an automobile accident. "You certainly don't deserve this," people said to him. He agreed but also realized that he had not deserved those three wonderful people in his life either. His loss was not fair, but, he reflected, neither was his happiness.

When the driver who had caused the accident was acquitted, Sittser was enraged. "I did not want revenge," he wrote, "but I did want justice so that the man . . . would pay the just penalty for his wrong doing."[8] But then he began to question his own assumptions about fairness and justice. "The problem of expecting to live in a perfectly fair world is that there is no grace in that world, for grace is grace only when it is undeserved."[9] He ended his story with the prayer, "God spare us a life of fairness! I would prefer to take my chances living in a universe in which I get what I do not deserve. That means that I will suffer loss, as I already have, but it also means I will receive mercy."[10]

My understanding of mercy as an integral part of justice was strengthened when I reread that passage in *The Merchant of Venice*. There I found another line that had not been part of my high school assignment:

[Mercy] is an attribute of God himself,
And earthly power doth then show likest God's
When mercy seasons justice.[11]

When mercy seasons justice, we have "restorative justice" rather than "retributive justice." Retributive justice is about retribution and punishment: "An eye for an eye and a tooth for a tooth" (Exodus 21:24). Those who seek vengeance seek retributive justice. Our prison systems are built on the concept of retributive justice, and the death penalty is our ultimate expression of retributive justice. Restorative justice, on the other hand, holds forth the possibility of reconciliation. "The chief concern of restorative justice," wrote Archbishop Desmond Tutu of South Africa, "is the healing of breaches, redressing of imbalances, the restoration of broken relationships, a seeking to rehabilitate both the victim and the perpetrator."[12] Restorative justice is the way of the peacemakers.

Blessed Are the Peacemakers

One day when I was teaching fifth grade, my students came in red-faced and angry. I could see the sign of tears on some of their faces. But they came into the classroom quietly, for we had talked often about leaving the playground issues outside so that we could be about the business of learning. The boys and girls got out their math books, checked the assignment on the board, and started to work. All were in their seats. No one was talking or even whispering. All seemed peaceful, but I could sense powerful emotions simmering beneath the surface. I was in charge of that classroom. I could continue to keep the peace. The students could go on with their work and their good behavior. Or, I realized, I could become a peacemaker—a much more challenging proposition. I chose the latter by interrupting the silence. "Okay," I said, "What happened out there?" The peace of the classroom was shattered. Hands flew up, children yelled and flung accusations at one another. One student began to cry. I became engaged in the work of peacemaking.

In the gospel of Matthew, Jesus calls the people to be peacemakers. Jesus himself was a peacemaker, not a peace-keeper. This distinction helps us to understand his statement that he came not to bring peace but the sword (Matthew 10:34). When Jesus called the religious leaders of his day to repent the wrong they were doing to others, he raised a sword to the establishment. His was not a sword of violence; it was the sword of truth. And that truth upset the status quo. Jesus' sword called others to awareness and into radical action on behalf of social justice.[13] In the gospel of Luke, Mary, the mother of Jesus, foretold Jesus' call to create peace and systemic justice when she sang: "He has shown strength with his arm; he has scattered the proud in the thoughts of their hearts. He has brought down the powerful from their thrones, and lifted up the lowly; he has filled the hungry with good things, and sent the rich away empty" (Luke 1:51–53).

We too are called to be peacemakers, not only in our personal lives but in the whole world. We may long for personal peace and sometimes even experience a moment when peace graciously descends. I experienced that grace on those rare evenings after a hectic day when my children were small. With both boys finally in bed and asleep and the last load of laundry gently drying, I sat wondrously still and was filled with gratitude. Surely that was the blessing of peace, but it was not *shalom*—a Hebrew word that indicates a much bigger idea. Shalom is not only about individual peace but about peace for the community and peace for the world. As theologian Walter Brueggeman has said:

> If there is to be shalom, it will not be just for isolated, insulated individuals; it is rather, security and prosperity granted to a whole community—young and old, rich and poor, powerful and dependent. Always we are all in it together. Together we stand before God's blessing and together we receive the gift of life, if we receive it at all. Shalom comes only to the inclusive, embracing community that excludes none.[14]

When our lives are orderly and predictable, when we experience more pleasure than pain, when we feel we are in charge of things, we may breathe a prayer of gratitude and add the request, "Please God, let this peace remain." Yet in those delicious personal moments we may not recognize that the systems that contribute to our peace may be oppressive to others. The pleasures we find in our purchases may be the result of tragic working conditions on the other side of the world. The satisfaction we get at work may be at the expense of other workers in the same company. Personal peace and an orderly life may feel good, but they are not shalom, for shalom does not bring everything to rest; it puts everything in motion. Shalom does not prevent all risks but accepts every risk that is necessary for its work. Shalom does not resolve every conflict; rather, it accepts conflict as the context in which the work of shalom must be done. Peace is shalom only when it comes with and through justice.[15]

Peace with justice is a work in progress and attests to God's good will and transformative engagement for the sake of the world.[16] This is the promise that the prophet Jeremiah proclaimed:

> For surely I know the plans I have for you, says the Lord, plans for your welfare and not for harm, to give you a future with hope. Then when you call upon me and come and pray to me, I will hear you. When you search for me, you will find me: if you seek me with all your heart, I will let you find me, says the Lord, and I will restore your fortunes and gather you from all the nations and all the places where I have driven you, says the Lord, and I will bring you back to the place from which I sent you into exile (29:11–14).

Peace with and through justice in its fullest sense functions as a theology of hope, "a large-scale promissory vision of what will one day surely be."[17] To embrace a theology of hope, we must recognize that the search for peace and the search for justice are intertwined. We must not tolerate injustice for the sake of peace. We must not settle for peace for some individuals while others are at war. God's promise of shalom is for the world. We share in that promise by grounding ourselves in God through prayer and by doing what we can to make the promissory vision a reality.

Grounded in God

Just as the quest for justice and peace are intertwined, prayer and the work for justice and peace belong together. If we attempt this work on our own without the help of God, we may begin to believe that the vision of a just and peaceable kingdom is our own. Without a connection to God, we run the risk of following our own path and acting for our own glory. Grounding ourselves in God through prayer holds us accountable for our actions and keeps us connected to God's promise for the world and to God's desire for our role in creating that world. Our intimate relationship with God reminds us to pray with courageous spirits, clear minds, and merciful hearts. Through the five forms of prayer that follow, we can discover direction and receive the courage and strength to proceed in our prayers and actions for a just and peaceful world.

CHAPTER TWO

PRAYING FOR OTHERS AND THE WORLD

History belongs to the intercessors who believe the future into being.
—WALTER WINK

People from a number of churches in the same geographical area gathered to talk about intercessory prayer and to hold an ecumenical prayer service. After I had spoken with them regarding their assumptions about prayer, I asked them to remember times in their lives when they had prayed for someone else or a time when someone had prayed for them. I asked them to remember the experience and what had happened.

In the sharing, I heard many stories. "When my mother had cancer I prayed for her to be cured," a woman said. "The cancer didn't go away, but before she died our troubled relationship was healed."

A man spoke up: "When I was going into surgery, I knew my friends were praying for me. I imagined their prayers floating gently around me. I was comforted."

"I am praying that my son will find a job," a father shared. "I've been praying a long time. It's hard when my prayers are not answered, but I keep on praying."

After we had shared these personal stories of prayer, I asked them about praying for people further away. How might they pray for countries at war, victims of violence, refugees, the homeless, and the hungry? Could they pray for people and situations, even if they did not know very much about the issue? Could they pray for people without a clear idea of what those people needed? "I am concerned about the hungry people of our world," a woman said. "I weep over the pictures of starving children. I know how to pray for individuals in my life and even for groups of people I am part of, like my congregation or my community. But all the hungry, starving people of the world? I don't know what to do."

When we imagine praying for *shalom*—for justice and peace in the world—it is natural for us to feel overwhelmed in the face of such a huge task. We know how to pray for loved ones, for situations in which we are directly involved. I know how to pray for my friend in her struggle with addiction, how to pray for the healing of the conflict in my congregation, how to pray for the seminary as it seeks new leadership. I have a personal context for all these prayers. I can visualize the people, feel the struggle and the pain. I am often hopeful that there will be healing, resolution, and eventual well-being. But how and where do I begin with the enormous issues of starvation, homelessness, oppression, and war?

Start with the Heart

There is no way to make these world problems small enough to be manageable. Instead, we must begin within ourselves, in our own hearts. You may not feel you know how to pray, but you can still open your heart to God: "God, I want to pray for the starving people of the world. I don't know how to begin. Help me!" Perhaps you are angry that there is so much wrong in the world. Bring that anger into your prayer: "How can you let this happen, God? You who are a God of peace! Use your power! Use your wrath! Make them stop the killing!" Maybe you don't even know what to pray for because a situation is so confusing. You can give that to God as well: "I don't know what the refugees of the world need, Loving God. I only know they need you." If your own problems fill your heart and mind so that you cannot reach beyond them, you can take that struggle to God: "I need help right now, God. Be with me so I can find my way out of the darkness." You don't have to figure out how to pray before you begin. If you try to, you are leaving God out of the process. When you open your heart to God, you start to pray, allowing God to help you continue those prayers, gently change your prayers, and ultimately transform your heart.

A woman I know began to pray for peace in the Middle East. Anne had studied the problems there and felt strongly about how the situation should be resolved. She began her prayers where her heart was, telling God exactly what to do to bring about peace. She prayed angrily and insistently for a long time and then saw what she was actually doing:

> Through my specific, insistent form of prayer, I had put myself in control of the issue. I had defined the problem, I had identified the enemy, I had determined the proper solution and I was demanding that God create my preconceived solution. God had simply become an instrument of my will. When I realized what I had been doing, I put aside my demanding prayers and I began to pray prayers of surrender, prayers that lifted the Middle East conflict and all people affected by it into God's presence for God's solution.[1]

When her prayers changed, so did her heart. Anne was humbled by her arrogance and filled with gratitude that she had been led to surrender. The experience of surrender in prayer taught her the possibility of surrendering to God's guidance in other areas of her life.

Robert, a young man studying for the ministry, had a similar experience. He was worried about all the illnesses that were plaguing people he loved. He began by praying that the illnesses be taken away. "But prayers to take the illnesses away seemed like my agenda, not necessarily God's," he told me. "I slowly began to realize I needed a prayer not against the diseases but for the people who suffered them. I needed a prayer that would surround them with God's healing power."

Over the course of several days, Robert developed a prayer that he could say over and over again:

O, Lord, the unwell—make them well
O, Lord, the broken—make them whole
O, Lord, the hurting—ease their pain
O, Lord, send your healing spirit.[2]

He began by visualizing the people he knew who suffered illness, but soon his prayer expanded to include all people everywhere who were unwell, broken, and hurting. Then the prayer grew to include all people who cared for the ill and those working to discover cures. The prayer that had started out so specific grew and grew until it became a song in his heart that matched the rhythm of his breathing and became for him a prayer of hope. God had led Robert from his personal prayer to a prayer for a large group of unknown people. He was praying for peace and justice in the world.

Intercessory prayer is as important on the front lines of the struggle for justice and peace as it is for those who are safe at home. In 1980, peace activist Dorothy Friesen and her husband went to the Philippines to be in solidarity with suffering people in that nation.[3] Their neighbors were squatters with no secure homes and no money for food. People they knew were arrested, tortured, and killed. In the face of violence that was fueled by the military and supported by the American government, the Friesens were almost afraid to pray. She wrote:

> Broken, angry, and confused, we held these problems up to the light. But we had hesitations about prayer. We did not want to slip into magic or mail-order prayers, which would simply send up an order to have the goods delivered. Partly, we did not even know what to ask for. We did not know how to pray. We could only offer up our confusion. As we did that, we began to realize that it was not our definition or assessment of the problem which was determinative. When we place ourselves in the presence of God, a transformation takes place. Who God is becomes important. Emptying ourselves so that we may take in the person of God becomes the essential thing. It shapes our view of the situation; it shapes the nature of our involvement.[4]

What does Friesen mean when she says that we are to empty ourselves to take in the person of God? The easiest way for me to think about this possibility is to imagine a room filled with stuff—too much furniture, pictures covering all the walls, boxes of clothes and old toys piled in the corners, and books and magazines on every surface waiting to be read. One can only stand at the door and wonder, for there is no room to enter. Our hearts are often like that room—so full there is no room for God. Emptying means being willing to let go of the clutter, to throw out or give away what is no longer necessary externally and internally. We are to save only that which is essential and then step aside to make space for God. As Angelus Silesius, a Renaissance Christian mystic, wrote:

> God whose love and joy are everywhere
> can't come to visit
> unless you aren't there.[5]

Starting where their hearts were, Dorothy Friesen and others in her community began to pray by offering up their confusion. God led them to a prayer of emptying. However, this is not everyone's path. Another woman named Gretchen had her prayers changed in a different way when she went on a mission to Iraq to personally deliver medical supplies that had been blocked by American economic sanctions. Initially, she prayed for herself and the group she was going with. She prayed for courage, safety, and the ability to make a difference. While in Iraq, Gretchen let go of those specific requests and began to pray each day to be a channel of love to the people she encountered. When she returned home, she prayed for the individuals she had met, particularly for the children whose faces were etched on her heart. "And now," Gretchen said, "I pray for a whole people. I don't ask God to do this or that. I surround the people of Iraq with the light of God's love and imagine them becoming a channel for that love."

Another way to understand intercessory prayer is to imagine taking people and concerns into our hearts and then taking our hearts into the heart of God through meditation and silent prayer. In this prayer, we sit in the presence of God not asking, not telling, not confessing, not praising, not worshiping but simply consenting to God's desire to be with us. Mother Teresa of Calcutta described this prayer of consent as a prayer of listening. When asked what she said to God when she prayed, she replied, "Nothing. I only listen." "And what does God say?" "Nothing," she answered. "God only listens."[6] Understanding the power of silence in prayers of intercession helps me realize what Buddhist monk and peace activist Thich Nhat Hanh meant when he wrote, "Meditation is meditation for all of us."[7] It also gives poignancy to the words of the young man who said, "I pray with feelings. God allows me to feel the pain of the world. I have a talent for weeping."

Pray for Those Who Persecute You

As we learn to expand our prayers from the personal to the global, praying for people of the world as well as for our loved ones, we are offered another challenge in our prayers for justice and peace. Jesus invites us to pray for our enemies as well.

Jesus' commandment to "love your enemies and pray for those who persecute you" (Matthew 5:44) is a difficult one. Rarely do we respond, "OK, I'll do that." More likely we try to avoid it. We ignore the commandment or decide Jesus could not be speaking to us. We may feel that praying for our enemies will keep us from speaking out against an unjust situation. We may believe we are being asked to accept or condone what our enemies have done. We may even be confused about who our enemies are or whether we have any enemies. It is hard to know how to begin if we want to be faithful to this challenging commandment.

When I give a lecture titled "Praying for Friends and Enemies," I tell the audience that the Aramaic word that is commonly translated as "enemy" in the Bible can mean "someone with whom we are out of step."[8] One woman who had told me before the program that she had no enemies came to me afterward and said, "When I said I had no enemies, I was thinking of people who were out to get me, to do me bodily harm. I really don't have any of those in my life. But people with whom I am out of step! Oh, my! I have plenty of those."

Many of us can identify with this woman's sentiments, for we most likely know people with whom we are out of step. But in addition, we may also have people in our lives who are threatening us with psychological or physical violence. Victims of domestic abuse, those being sexually harassed, people in jobs where they are constantly being demeaned—all these people have enemies of a more serious nature. If we move from our personal world to the global community, we find enemies easily: rulers who steal money from their people, governments that imprison and torture people who disagree with them, those who sell women and children into prostitution, suicide bombers and assassins and those who send them, heads of corporations who care only for money and not for the welfare of their workers—all these and many more we can name are the enemies of justice and peace. Does Jesus really mean we are supposed to pray for them?

People who are engaged in intercessory prayers for justice and peace tell me again and again that when they start praying for the victims in an unjust situation, they end up praying for the oppressors as well. "As I prayed for victims of domestic violence," one man said, "I was led to read more about the reality of those caught in this vicious cycle. I learned that most abusers had been abused themselves. My heart opened to them and I included them in my prayers." And a woman told me: "When I prayed for the oppressed people of Chiapas, I realized my prayers were incomplete without praying for the people who kept the unjust system in place. Without a change of heart leading to a change of behavior, there seems to be no hope for justice. I must pray for them."

Praying for our enemies can grow out of our prayers for the dispossessed, the hungry, the marginalized. Or praying for our enemies can come from love and our understanding that God loves all of us, good and bad, victim and oppressor, weak and strong. In her memoir, novelist A. Manette Ansay wrote of her experience as a young girl praying for the biggest enemy she could think of—Satan.

> *Dear God,* I plead with the dark emptiness above my bed, *I'm sorry for all my sins. Please bless my mother and brother and father and me, and people here and on other planets, and all animals everywhere—*
> I say the same thing every night, though "all the animals everywhere" is a recent addition. Father Stone says that animals can't go to heaven, but I believe that if I pray, if I have faith, all things are possible.
> *And please protect everybody who has died, and everybody who hasn't been born yet, and Satan—*
> After all, didn't God say to love all things? And wasn't Satan one of his creatures? I have an idea that if everybody prays for him, Satan will come around to God's light once again, wake up as if splashed by cold water, and then there will be no more evil in the world. For a while I'd been enlisting the help of kids at school, making them join hands to pray for Satan in the belly of the jungle gym, but then my teacher gave me a note, in a sealed envelope, to take home to my mother. So now, I pray for Satan in the privacy of my bedroom.[9]

We can learn a lot from this little girl's faith and trust in God. She knows that heaven is available to all God's creatures and that no one is excluded from God's mercy. If we substitute the name of our greatest enemy for the name of Satan, we might ask, as she did, "Isn't he or she one of God's creatures?" And I love the idea that my greatest enemy could "wake up as if splashed by cold water" and come willingly into God's light. But praying for our enemies is not popular, as Ansay discovered, and it is usually even less welcome if the enemy is near rather than far away.

Having the courage to pray for an enemy whose violence and oppression was felt daily is the lesson Elias Chacour, Palestinian Christian peace worker, learned from his father. He wrote of his father's words to his family after soldiers had destroyed his livelihood: "'Children,' his father said softly, turning those sad eyes upon us, 'if someone hurts you, you can curse him. But that would be useless. Instead, you have to ask the Lord to bless the man who makes himself your enemy. And do you know what will happen? The Lord will bless you with inner peace—and perhaps your enemy will turn from his wickedness. If not, the Lord will deal with him.'"[10]

Night after night, Elias would hear the words of his father's prayer: "Forgive them O God, heal their pain. Remove their bitterness. Let us show them your peace."[11]

If love and compassion do not motivate us to pray for our enemies, as they did for Elias Chacour's father, we can turn inward and let our hearts guide us in prayer. But what if we do so and find that our hearts are filled with anger? Can we pray from our anger? The psalmist did. In Psalm 137, he raged and cried out to God against the Edomites who had destroyed his beloved city, Jerusalem.

Remember, O Lord, against the Edomites
the day of Jerusalem's fall,

How they said, "Tear it down! Tear it down!
Down to its foundations!"
O daughter of Babylon, you devastator!
Happy shall they be who pay you back
what you have done to us!
Happy shall they be who take your little ones
And dash them against the rock! (137:7–9)

When we cry out our anger in prayer, God hears, recognizes, and honors the rage in our hearts but will not let us remain there. When we are naked in our honesty, God will guide us to more gentle forms of prayer.

Years ago, I spoke with a man whose sister had been randomly attacked and raped. He was filled with rage. "I prayed the Psalms for weeks," he told me. "I raged and wept and told God what I wanted done to the man who had done this horrible thing." One day as he was praying his rage, it suddenly came to him that this man had a family and that family was also grieving. "My heart softened," he said. "I felt the pain of that other family and I began to pray for them." He was never able to pray for the rapist directly, but the prayers for the rapist's family allowed the rage and desire for revenge to fade. He could lovingly support his sister as she found healing and could be with her when she appeared in court to identify her attacker.

Sometimes, wordless prayers are a way to pray for your enemies. You can simply lift the person or the people up to God. To do this, imagine you are holding in your hands the one with whom you are out of step. Using your body, raise your arms and hands as high as you can reach, as if you were lifting the person into the presence of God. Hold him or her there for a moment, then open your hands and let the person go into God's loving care. As you allow your hands to return to your sides, feel the experience of release. When resentment, bitterness, and anger return, you can pray this prayer again—holding, lifting, and releasing—until your heart softens and your prayers are transformed.

Lois, a student in seminary, decided to pray for Osama bin Laden following the September 11, 2001, terrorist attacks in the United States and discovered this prayer form for herself. She made her commitment in the context of a class assignment to choose one issue of justice and peace to pray about daily for the ten weeks of the course. The students had a week to reflect and to decide where they would focus their prayers of intercession. At the beginning of the following class, I asked them to share one at a time who or what they would be praying for. Lois told me later that she had been surprised by her decision to pray for Osama bin Laden. "When you asked us to share our prayer commitments, I hadn't made up my mind. When it was my turn to speak, his name just popped out of my mouth. I knew I would have no prayer words to utter. I realized that all I could do was to hold him up to the love of God."

As the class paused to reflect on the wide variety of prayer commitments, one woman said, "I am grateful someone is praying for Osama bin Laden. I know I can't." There was a murmur of agreement and appreciation from other students. "I felt their support for my difficult prayer," Lois said. "It made it easier in subsequent weeks to raise him into the presence of God. Sometimes he felt so heavy I could hardly lift him, but I knew I was being supported by my classmates."

One day when she was praying, Osama bin Laden seemed particularly difficult to lift. She remembered a phrase from an old song: "He ain't heavy, he's my brother." Lois was overcome by the grace of that insight. In praying for the enemy, her heart had been transformed.

"I cannot think of him as I did before. I read the newspapers differently. He is still the enemy of my country. And he is my brother."

When we pray for our enemies, we do not give up our stance for justice and peace. Our prayers do not mean that we condone unjust behavior. As Martin Luther King Jr. taught, "Praying for one's enemies need not lead to a quiescent politics; such praying reminds us that one may contend sharply with the unjust enemy yet still leave him room to turn around."[12] Praying for our enemies is not passive, nor do our prayers condone evil. Praying for our enemies brings mercy and hope for transformation to places of tyranny, war, and oppression.

In the gospel of Luke, Jesus concludes his teachings on the treatment of enemies with these words: "But love your enemies, do good, and lend, expecting nothing in return. Your reward will be great, and you will be children of the Most High; for he is kind to the ungrateful and the wicked. Be merciful, just as your Father is merciful" (Luke 6:35–36). To follow this commandment, we turn to God in prayer, for we cannot love the ungrateful and the wicked without God's help. As author and Roman Catholic priest Joseph Nassal said, "It is only through the power of God's mercy that we will ever find the courage to be merciful ourselves."[13]

Knock Incessantly and Persevere

Intercessory prayer is hard work and not for the faint at heart. We cry out to God constantly to end the violence, to bring justice to all people, to lift up the fallen, to heal the sick and the brokenhearted. We are asking for no less than to see the reign of God become a reality. We do not offer our prayers a few times and then let them go. As John Calvin wrote, "We must repeat the same supplications not twice or three times only, but as often as we have need, a hundred and a thousand times. We must never be weary in waiting for God's help."[14]

When Calvin uses the term *supplication,* he is referring to a particularly intense and sustained form of intercessory prayer—one that writer and teacher Richard Foster described: "Supplication means to ask with earnestness, with intensity, and with perseverance. It is a declaration that we are deadly serious about this prayer business. We are going to keep at it and not give up."[15] Think of the parable of the man at midnight who desired bread to show hospitality to his friend (Luke 11:5–8). He did not knock once and take no for an answer. He knocked again and again. I imagine his knocking turning to pounding on the door. He was determined not to go away empty-handed. Remember also the parable of the widow who went to the judge seeking justice (Luke 18:1–5). He had no interest in serving justice, but he finally responded to her pleas so she would not wear him out by continually appearing. These stories tell us to knock incessantly, beg continually, and persevere in our prayers.

Supplications are not quiet prayers offered in poetic form. They are not offered in subdued voices. Rather, they are loud and raucous. As writer and professor Walter Wink says, "Biblical prayer is impertinent, persistent, shameless, indecorous. It is more like haggling in an outdoor bazaar than the polite monologues of the churches."[16] A powerful example of haggling with God is the story of Abraham arguing against the Lord's decision to completely destroy the city of Sodom (Genesis 18). Abraham stands before the Lord and says, "Will you indeed sweep away the righteous with the wicked: Suppose there are fifty righteous within the city; will you then sweep away the place and not forgive it for the fifty righteous who are in it?" (Genesis 18:23–24). The Lord agrees that if fifty righteous are found, he will forgive the whole city for their sake. Then Abraham asks for forty-five, then forty, then thirty, then twenty; finally, he bargains the Lord down to ten righteous people. The Lord agrees and says, "For the sake of them I will not destroy it" (Genesis 18:32). Might we be as bold as Abraham in our prayers for justice and mercy!

Answered and Unanswered Prayers

As we pray from our hearts, as we pray for our enemies, as we experience being broken open and our lives transformed, what of the people and places and situations for which we are praying? We know without a doubt that prayer transforms the one who prays, but what do we do when wars continue to wage, tyrants remain in power, and children die of starvation? Are our prayers doing any good? Is God really listening? Where is God's radical intervention that will change the face of the world?

Walter Wink tells us that God is close to us and involved in creation and that when we pray for peace and justice and liberation, God hears our prayers. But "God's ability to intervene . . . is sometimes tragically restricted in ways we cannot pretend to understand. It takes considerable spiritual maturity to live in the tension between these two facts: God has heard our prayer, and the Powers are blocking God's response."[17]

The Powers that Wink is referring to are the structures and institutions that exploit, oppress, and perpetuate injustice in the world. The Powers are systems that emerge and grow over time through a series of individual and collective decisions until the systems become so large that no one individual is in control. The Powers may have begun as benign structures to help people live more effectively in community, but the Powers can lose their original intent and grow unchecked into systems that become capable of evil.[18] But the Powers' capacity for oppression and injustice is not more powerful than God's will to good.

Just as God's power has always been limited by the freedom of will that God granted humankind, so God's power is limited by the freedom of institutions and systems.[19] I have the choice to treat other people with kindness or cruelty. God gave me that freedom. Institutions make decisions that honor people or oppress people. God gave them that freedom as well, for the Powers are part of God's creation. "The Powers are inextricably locked into God's system. . . . They are answerable to God. And that means that every subsystem in the world is, in principle, redeemable. Nothing is outside the redemptive care and transforming love of God."[20]

And so we pray. Boldly, loudly, persistently, relentlessly, knowing that anything and everything is possible with God. The Powers may temporarily thwart God's response to our prayers, but not forever. The Powers may stand in the way of God's saving action, but not forever. Ultimately God will prevail.[21]

Philosopher Douglas Steere contends that prayers of intercession lower the threshold in the person or people or system prayed for "to make the besieging love of God . . . slightly more visible and more inviting."[22] With this image, we can have faith that our radical prayers for justice and the transformation of the Powers are lowering thresholds in systems and institutions and in individual hearts. I believe that is what happened in South Africa.

One of the most oppressive and evil systems of recent years was South African apartheid. In existence for decades, everyone suffered from it and few took responsibility for it. For years, those who tried to change the system were killed or imprisoned. There seemed no end to the violence. Yet people throughout the world continued to pray. They were praying that justice would come to that beleaguered nation and its people. Over time, the possibility of another way was envisioned. God's love became visible and inviting. When apartheid finally ended and the nation held open and free elections, Archbishop Desmond Tutu proclaimed that apartheid would never have ended without the persistent prayers of the people of the world.

Walter Wink calls intercession the politics of hope.[23] People who engage in intercessory prayer are instruments of that hope. To pray for others and the world means that we have a vision of the future. It requires us to believe the impossible is possible. It demands that we live in this moment as if the future were already here. When we engage in intercessory prayer, we become prophetic—a truth that Richard Foster said so well: "The true prophetic message always calls us to stretch our arms out wide and embrace the whole world. In holy boldness we cover the earth with the grace and the mercy of God."[24]

An Invitation to Pray

Think of a world situation that is in need of prayer, such as a place where war rages, where injustice rules, or where poverty, illness, or hunger is the norm. Choose an issue that touches your heart as well as your mind, and make a commitment to pray for the people in that place every day for a month. Start where your heart is and persevere in prayer. Let yourself be guided by the spirit, and notice how your prayer changes over the weeks. Pay attention to any way your prayer expands to include all involved, even those you may hold accountable for the situation. Remember that as you pray, you are joining others around the world in many cultures and traditions who are also praying for justice and peace.

CHAPTER THREE

PRAYING WITH OUR ACTIONS

Almost anything you do will seem insignificant, but it is
very important that you do it.
—GANDHI

In the fellowship hall of a small inner-city United
Methodist Church in Denver, a group of people in their
elder years talked and laughed as they clipped coupons from
the newspaper as part of a service project for an ecumenical
group called Capitol Hill United Ministries (CHUM). After
the coupons were cut, sorted, and folded, they would be
placed on items in a local supermarket. If customers bought
items with coupons attached, they had two choices: to simply use the coupons to save money on the products they
were purchasing or to tell the clerk to donate the value of
the coupon to CHUM. This simple activity—small as it
may be—contributes to a just and peaceful world.

Started almost twenty years ago and known locally as
the Coupon Project, this group has raised over $300,000 that
is granted to local organizations that serve the people of
Capitol Hill. The grants from the project aid many grass-
roots organizations that serve the city's most vulnerable
people—children and youth, and those who are homeless,
abused, and chronically mentally ill.

The day I visited, those gathered were eager to talk to
me as they worked and to tell me what the project meant to
them. "This is service work that calls for the greatest faith,"
one woman said, "for we never see the people we serve. We
can only trust that our work here makes a difference."

"Doing for others is part of my faith," a man added, "and now that I am old there are things I can no longer do. This I can do, and I thank God for the opportunity to continue to serve."

They were intrigued with the idea that what they were doing as they worked and told stories could be considered prayer. "Oh no," one ninety-year-old woman laughed. "This isn't prayer. I just do this because in my family I was told that if something was not right I should do something or shut up about it. That's why I'm here."

"Praying," another woman murmured thoughtfully. "I don't know. When I moved to Denver after I was widowed, I knew no one. I thought I had come here to die. And then I found the Coupon Project and I am very much alive. Could my very life be a prayer?"

"I know I offer continual prayers of gratitude," a woman shared. "I have been of service since I started volunteering with my mother at the Red Cross when I was seven. Eighty years later I am still working for justice and peace. That's a lot to be thankful for."

"Service could be prayer," another woman added. "A prayer with no words." From across the room a man shouted, "Oh no, this couldn't be prayer. We're having too much fun!" They all hooted with laughter.

Laughter, gratitude, and trust are all part of praying with our actions. And love is the heart of our action prayers. The people of CHUM come faithfully every week, motivated by their love of God, each other, and the unknown people they serve. In their own quiet way, they are similar to the people in the little village of Le Chambon-sur-Lignon who welcomed Jews and others fleeing from the Nazis during World War II. At great risk to themselves, they offered a warm welcome and refuge to all in need. In trying to determine what led these people to their acts of mercy, one man who heard their stories wrote: "While there is no single explanation for their actions . . . the most important fact for us to know is that they were brought up to understand all the idioms of the language of love. When their hearts spoke to them, they first listened, then they acted."[1]

Motivated by Love

Mother Teresa told the people who served with her in Calcutta, "Don't look for spectacular actions; what is important is the gift of yourselves. It is the degree of love you insert in your deeds."[2] Without love, our actions may be motivated by power, self-righteousness, pity, or guilt and will separate us from the love and mercy of God in whose name we act. Motivated by love for God and neighbor, our intention and attention are with God, and our activities for justice and peace become a prayer.

In 1982, a community dedicated to nonviolent direct action in response to nuclear arms proliferation named themselves the Agape Community. Part of their statement of purpose read: "We believe the spiritual force capable of both changing us and stopping the arms race is that of agape: the love of God operating in the human heart."[3] This community began to keep track of the trains carrying nuclear weapons and organized demonstrations and prayer vigils at key places along the routes. Critical to their vision of stopping the trains was agape, realized through prayer. Agape turned their nonviolent actions into prayer.

Agape was at the heart of the Coupon Project and in the hearts of the people of Le Chambon-sur-Lignon; it gave hope to the community dedicated to nonviolent direct action. And agape led Carter Case and her husband Steve to South Africa two years after Steve had been diagnosed with

HIV. When he received the diagnosis, both were terrified, angry, and confused. Love and service were far from their thoughts. However, as time passed, they were ready to share their experience with family, friends, and colleagues. They began to realize the power of storytelling to transform hearts. They spoke to church gatherings, school programs, and health care facilities. "Storytelling became a prayer," Carter said. "Our story put a face on AIDS and helped us to connect to others and to God."

Carter and Steve decided to take their prayers to a region where silence about the disease was the norm. They learned of a small village where HIV-positive women were involved in an embroidery project to help support themselves and their families. Carter and Steve commissioned a large tapestry and then traveled to South Africa to meet the women and share stories with them. Their own willingness to share broke down barriers, and many women spoke openly for the first time. "We did not choose this journey," Carter and Steve told me, "but the experience of living with HIV has transformed our lives. We do what we can from the blessings of love we have received from God, from friends, and from strangers."

As travel and listening and storytelling became a prayer for Carter and Steve, so any action, as insignificant as it may seem, can become a prayer. How does that happen? How do we find the love to motivate us? How do we connect to God in the midst of our activities?

Intention and Attention

When love guides our intention to dedicate our work to God, to find God in all we do and say, to allow God to direct our actions and our speech, our justice and peace efforts become prayers. A woman named Emily shared her experience of turning an ordinary activity into a prayer for justice and peace.

"I have been active in my church's program to help homeless families," Emily said. "For one week a month these families eat and sleep in our church. I have grown to love the people I have met through our ministry, and I wanted to share this love with the children of our congregation. One of our Sunday School classes was planning on making Christmas boxes for the homeless families, so I asked their teacher if I could come and talk to them before they began their project. I really wanted to make my presentation a prayer, so I prayed before the presentation. I prayed as I walked in the door. And then I forgot all about God as I spoke to my young audience. I was so intent on finding the right words to help them know the depth and seriousness of homelessness that God went right out of my mind."

When she shared her story with her prayer group, one member responded, "It still seems like a prayer to me. In the classroom, you needed to attend to the children before you. That didn't mean your heart was not attending to God." Another woman concurred. "We don't have to be praying with words as we act and speak to make what we are doing a prayer. Your intention and the loving attention you have given to the homeless and then to the children in the class made your presentation a prayer." A man put it slightly differently: "I think your love and the quality of your presence made your presentation a prayer."

Upon hearing these reflections, Emily said, "Maybe you're right. Maybe I was praying. And I now remember something the teacher said to me when I left. She told me that she had never experienced this particular group of children so quiet and attentive. She said she thought I had captured their hearts." The prayer group reflected quietly on this discussion and the ideas Emily's experience presented. Then one student spoke into the silence: "I think that our task is to bring love, intention, and attention to our actions. When we do this, God will turn our actions into prayers. We don't make our actions prayer; God does."

For God to transform our actions into prayers, we need to surrender to the grace and mercy of God and allow God to work first in our hearts and then through our actions. Nowhere is this more important than when we take our action prayers into the public arena.

Going to Jail for Justice

Kate Stevens, a pastor and organic farmer, felt called to Washington, D.C., to pray publicly at the Department of Energy concerning the proposal to drill for oil in the Arctic coastal plain.[4] She joined 150 others to "pray and sing for the earth. We prayed for the President and the workers at the Department of Energy and we prayed for ourselves, recognizing that any change we worked for had to begin with changing our own consumptive ways of living."[5] At the end of worship, twenty-two of the group, with Kate among them, went to the entrance and knelt to pray out loud in a variety of languages and from many different religious traditions. They were warned they were breaking the law, but they remained in prayer. After the third warning, they were arrested and taken in police vans to spend fifteen hours in jail. Kate wrote of her experience: "I will never forget that day because my heart was broken open. I prayed like I have never prayed before. I was aware of my connection with all the earth and with all its peoples."[6]

Kate and her colleagues were engaged in civil disobedience, for they were putting their obedience to conscience and to God ahead of obedience to human law. An act of civil disobedience is sometimes based on the personal convictions that to obey an unjust law would violate one's faithfulness to God. At other times, it is a political action designed to bring about social change. Often the action is a combination of inward faithfulness and desire for a new reality.[7] Gandhi described civil disobedience "as the necessary resistance a good person must give to an evil government or law. It was both a way for the individual to draw closer to God, the source of all goodness, and a way for a whole people to . . . set in motion vast forces of positive social change."[8]

Learning from the wisdom and activities of Gandhi, Martin Luther King Jr. taught and used the tactics of civil disobedience in the struggle for civil rights. Its effectiveness there served as an inspiration for the later resistance to the Vietnam War and still later in protests against the nuclear arms race. Nonviolent civil disobedience continues to be used when people of conscience prayerfully decide that a law leads to injustice, discrimination, and oppression.

Integral to acts of civil disobedience are prayer and love. Gandhi wrote that "disobedience combined with love is the living water of life."[9] The group Kate Stevens was part of prepared prayerfully and prayed publicly as part of their protest against the Department of Energy's drilling plan. Anti-war activist Jim Douglas has stated that acts of nonviolent civil disobedience can themselves be seen as prayer. But he warns that if not done with a loving spirit, with a willingness to see oneself as part of the problem, our acts of civil disobedience can become a battle and contribute to the violence we seek to overcome.[10]

Writer and activist Sister Cecily Jones tries to bring that loving spirit to all her actions for justice and peace. She also understands the temptations inherent in acts of civil disobedience. "People are always interested in my arrests and jail time," she told me. "I have been arrested six times and

EMBRACING THE WORLD

gone to jail twice. But that is a very small part of my ongoing work for justice and peace. I do attend many marches, demonstrations, and prayer vigils, but I also pray and write and make phone calls. Those quiet acts are just as important." Now in her seventies, Sister Cecily has learned that her actions for justice and peace are not about her own empowerment. She is simply following one of the mission statements of her religious order: "We work for justice and act for peace because the gospel urges us."[11] Her obedience to this guideline makes Sister Cecily's activities, whether private or public, prayerful actions for justice and peace.

Personal contact between people involved on both sides of an issue can also turn acts of civil disobedience into prayer. Action that keeps people apart, that is not compassionate, or that makes "the other" an enemy is not prayerful. When we strive to take the power away from another to empower ourselves, we are not agents of God's grace and mercy. Jim Douglas said, "A spiritually based nonviolence, one that truly seeks change from within, has to engage deeply the spirits of both sides of the conflict. . . . The most enduring thing we can achieve . . . is, in the end, our relationship to the people we touch and who touch us."[12]

United Nation's Ambassador Andrew Young's early experience at a jail in Albany, Georgia, illuminates the power of personal contact in the struggle for justice. Young, a close friend and colleague of Martin Luther King Jr., visited him regularly after King had been sentenced to forty-five days in jail. On his first visit, Young was met by a guard who used racial epithets to announce his visit to King. Young made no mention of the language, simply smiled at the guard, looked closely at his name tag, and went on to visit his friend. On his next visit, Young called the guard by name, talked about the weather, and learned of his family. In later visits, always calling the guard by name, he began to inquire about the guard's health and asked after his wife and children. The racial language continued for a while, lessened, and then stopped. Young wrote, "It was my father's teaching coming through—show compassion to those who have no idea how to behave properly."[13] Years later, the guard was able to report that the kind and compassionate treatment he received from Young had changed his life. Young had engaged the spirit of the other side of the conflict.

Young obeyed his father's teachings about compassion when he went to the Albany jail. Obedience to a higher authority, a deeper call, or a prompting of the heart is a necessary part of prayerful civil disobedience. Obedience was surely Sala Nolan's response to a phone call asking her to come to a prison in Oklahoma where Wanda Jean Allen was to be executed. "We need you here," her caller said. "We have no African American woman to bear witness." "I simply went," she told me. "I had no idea what to expect. I was called to serve." When Sala arrived, she was welcomed into the community of witnesses. They stood together in the pouring rain, singing and praying. When Wanda Jean was taken to the death house, Sala moved forward. "I did not go to Oklahoma to be arrested," she said. "I went to participate and lend support. But when the call came I went forward and I crossed the line. It was a spontaneous action, based on faith, following spirit. I felt relieved. I felt as if I had done what I was called to do. I came to bear witness, to spend the night in jail, to bond with those incarcerated."

In jail, she joined the other women in prayer and meditation. They shared stories, strong emotions, and hard questions. And while Sala was in jail, Wanda Jean Allen was executed. The witness and prayer vigil did not prevent her death. "But I did not do for naught," Sala said. "Connections were made. Something happened in Oklahoma. We cannot know the final effect of our actions. My path is simply to honor spirit and obey the call."

Prayerful acts of civil disobedience seek change in laws, government, or corporate practices. Prayerful activists bring their hope and their faith that the world can be transformed in accordance with God's law and promise of justice. They acknowledge that they are part of whatever problem they are confronting and that they can become part of the solution. These activists work and pray for specific changes. They see clearly what must be done. Of equal importance is another form of prayerful activism, when people go into conflicted, oppressive, and painful places with no plan of action and no idea of a solution. They go with empty hands and minds and hearts to simply be present to what is. This loving presence with no words, no actions, no agenda, and no resolution is what Zen teacher and peace activist Bernie Glassman calls "bearing witness."[14]

Bearing Witness

It is difficult to be in the presence of suffering and do nothing. If we cannot do something, we tend to turn away or stay away. We feel useless and powerless, and we want to run. Michelle Negron Bueno wrote of her experience of powerlessness in El Salvador after an earthquake buried many of her friend's family under twelve hundred feet of dirt, boulders, and debris. Each day she went with her friend to sit at the burial site, waiting for news. "Why am I here if I cannot truly help?" she wondered. After days of anguished waiting, before the bodies were recovered, Michelle felt the presence of God and heard the words, "I am with you. I was with them when they died, and I am here with you now."[15] Michelle was bearing witness. By her presence, she was bringing love to that place of grief.

Sister Renee was called to bear witness on death row when she read in a local paper that Greg, a former student, had been convicted of five murders and sentenced to death. "My heart demanded I write to him," she said. He responded, and for ten years she visited and corresponded with him on death row. She was often doubtful that she was doing anything to help. She did not know what he needed. He was unable to believe in a loving and forgiving God. But she continued to write and bear witness to his suffering.

Sister Renee's religious community was aware of her witness and supported her with prayers. In addition, they took a corporate and public stance against the death penalty. On the eve of the execution, the community held an open prayer service for Greg and his victims. In attendance was the family of one of those murdered who had walked the long and painful road to forgiveness. The victim's mother spoke to the assembled congregation, giving thanks for her daughter's life and offering prayers for Greg, asking God to help him know and believe that he was loved and forgiven.[16]

Bearing witness is about living with questions rather than answers, mystery rather than certainty, not knowing rather than knowing. In Zen Buddhism, this way of being is called living with beginner's mind. Beginner's mind allows us to be present to the situation with no idea of what will happen, what we should do, or how to change anything. Beginner's mind allows us to be fully present.

Might you be willing to practice beginner's mind? When you bear witness with beginner's mind, you are open and listen with your heart. Nothing more is asked of you than to know to your core what another is going through. You might bear witness privately as you sit silently and prayerfully with a dying friend or when you listen with loving attention to the stories of others. You might bear witness publicly if you stand outside a prison, join a prayer service in a migrant camp, or sit in the shadow of government buildings. What are you doing when you bear witness? Some would say you are doing nothing. But I believe that you are bringing the power of God's love and mercy to bear on the situation. God, through your witness, has the power to transform hearts and lives. Sometimes doing nothing lovingly makes something happen.

Letting Go and Staying Engaged

Those who bear witness and the prayerful activists who practice and support civil disobedience are all called to an attitude of nonattachment. In the Bhagavad Gita, a sacred text of Hinduism, we find these words: "Do your duty, always: but without attachment. This is how one reaches the ultimate truth; by working without anxiety about results."[17] Letting go of our attachment to arrive, to succeed, to make a difference is difficult in any situation, but it is particularly difficult in the work for justice and peace. We believe God wants a just and peaceful world; we are committed to making it happen. How can we let go of our attachment to success and at the same time stay engaged with the people and the situation before us?

Jewish theologian Martin Buber said that success is not a name of God. Mother Teresa of Calcutta told us that God calls us to be faithful, not successful. Lucia Guzman, a United Methodist minister, has learned to follow this wisdom. She has traded the pulpit in church for the pulpit of the streets in Denver's Hispanic community. Her extension ministry includes community organizing, advocacy, politics, peacemaking, and prayer—lots of prayer. "What I do is a prayer," she told me. "My prayer is my journey into areas of injustice." As Lucia witnesses daily to instances of violence and injustice, she often feels discouraged and angry.

But not for long. "If I respond from the anger, I shut off all communication and possibility of movement," she said. "But if I go into prayer, alone or with those who have been treated unjustly, we can acknowledge together the hurt and anger, turn it over to God, and then discover ways we can move forward with hope and celebration." Lucia said, "I know I won't live to see the full reign of God, or even to know the completion of an act of justice. But I see the small things that happen, and I celebrate the steps. And I trust that good will come about, justice will prevail, and the light will overcome the darkness."

Celebrating the small steps, as Lucia has learned to do, and trusting in the goodness and the mercy of God help us to take action without attaching ourselves to success. When we count on measurable success to keep us working for justice and peace, we quickly become discouraged, exhausted, and tempted to give up our work. When we look to the future and all that needs to be accomplished, we can be overwhelmed. Peacemaking is endless, but if we stay focused on the present, unattached to particular goals, we are not overcome by the enormity before us. We simply proceed one step at a time.

Moving slowly, celebrating, and trusting keeps us attentive to the present moment, opens our eyes to the possibilities along the way and the gifts before us. Presbyterian missionary Anne Sayre, who served in Guatemala for five years, found this to be true. One of her joys was working with a women's weaving collective to help them achieve some level of economic stability. "This is a long, slow road we are on," she told me. "If I worried about success, I would miss the deepening friendships, the smiles on the children's faces, the joy at the arrival of the new sewing machine, the pleasure of a shared meal. Each step forward lifts our spirits and keeps our hope alive. If we focus on the future, we get overwhelmed."

To work without attachment, both Lucia and Anne placed their focus on the people involved in their struggle for justice and on the God they serve. This was the message that Thomas Merton wrote in a letter to his friend Jim Forest.

> Do not depend on the hope of results. When you are doing the sort of work you have taken on, essentially an apostolic work, you may have to meet the fact that your work will be apparently worthless and achieve no result at all, if not perhaps results opposite to what you expect. As you get used to this idea, you start more and more to concentrate not on the results but on the value, the rightness, the truth of the work itself. And there too a great deal has to be gone through, as gradually you struggle less and less for an idea and more and more for specific people. The range tends to narrow down, but it gets more and more real. In the end, it is the reality of personal relationships that saves everything.[18]

When we attend to the personal relationships—the individuals before us—our focus shifts from the end result to the present moment. We are able to see the hope in the eyes of a homeless woman, feel the firm handshake of a prisoner, witness a policeman carefully tending an elderly woman he is arresting after she prayerfully stepped over the line onto government property. When we practice nonattachment, we attend to God in the present moment, stay connected to the people involved, and let go of our need for results and our desire for success. Nonattachment is not a static place at which we arrive and from which we live. Rather it is a dynamic way,[19] a dance between the opposite poles of attachment (totally enmeshed) and detachment (totally disengaged). Both poles have gifts to offer and dangers to avoid.

Attachment brings the gifts of engagement, passion, and risk. When I am writing a lecture, I am deeply attached to the ideas, to my desire to be clear and evocative, and to the group that will hear my presentation. This connection engages me with the material and the audience, gives passion to my words and delivery, and allows me to take risks in what I say and the stories I choose to tell. But if I become attached to having my words applauded, my ideas accepted, my lecture a roaring success, I have succumbed to the dangers of attachment—enmeshment, self-deception, and loss of vision. In the preparation and presentation of the lecture, I may become blind to the possibilities of the moment. I may choose stories that are safe and that I am sure the audience will like. I may become as pleasing as I can be so I will be loved. Attached to success, I will be less likely to speak my truth. When I become aware of the dangers of attachment, I counter my tendency to attachment by moving toward the opposite pole—detachment.

Detachment holds the gifts of perspective, clarity, and an opportunity for self-reflection. If you choose to serve abused women in the local safe house, you will need to be able to stand back and see clearly what the women are coping with and the reality of their situations. You will need to hear their stories and their feelings without drowning in them. You will need to be able to reflect on your own life and choices if you wish to understand the lives and choices of these women. But if you become too detached, your heart will harden; you may create a wall between yourself and those you serve, and you could begin to feel that their suffering is not your problem. If you become too detached, you will experience the dangers of this extreme and find yourself isolated, lacking compassion and avoiding responsibility. When this begins to happen, you can move back toward attachment to re-engage with the women you serve.

To live and serve with an attitude of nonattachment is to dance our way between attachment and detachment. It is a process and a practice. We pay attention to where we are, to what is happening in our hearts and minds; we notice if we are moving to one extreme or the other, then we gently correct ourselves toward the center. We accept the gifts from both sides of the polarity and dance away from the dangers. We are learning the dance of letting go and staying engaged. The more we are able to live from this dance, the more our words and actions can become prayers for justice and peace.

Finding Courage in Community

Praying with your actions and your voice can be solitary prayer. You may be alone when you speak out against racism; you may be the only person listening to a story of violence and oppression or closing yourself off from others for a week so you can write stories to educate others about issues of justice and peace. But praying with actions can also be corporate prayer. You might form a community to respond to the threat of nuclear war, gather a group to attend a prayer vigil, or enlist children in a Sunday School class to fill boxes for homeless families, as Emily did in her church. You might bear witness to the homeless, as one Episcopal parish did, with everyone traveling together to walk the streets and visit the shelters to open themselves to the desperate needs in the community.

Whether we pray alone or with others, community is imperative for our well-being. I have never met an activist who has not longed for, appreciated, and counted on the prayers and support of their communities. Cecily feels so supported by her religious community in her ministry of action and witness that she cannot imagine how anyone without community could do the endless task of peacemaking. "My community renews me, supports me, loves me," she said. "They have given me the courage to do what I do."

We can support one another in our congregations and communities by sharing our peace and justice concerns, reporting on actions we are taking, and asking for prayers. When Carter told her church about Steve's HIV diagnosis, she was not only seeking support for herself and Steve but she was raising the congregation's awareness of the pandemic in this country and in Africa. The congregation supported their trip with prayers and offerings. Part of Anne's ministry in Guatemala was to send a quarterly letter to congregations of the Presbyterian Church, USA, to keep people who supported the mission informed of activities, needs, and prayers.

When we don't have a ready community to call on for support, working and praying for justice and peace can feel lonely. You may feel frightened if you are writing a sermon that calls for peaceful solutions when you know many in your congregation are in favor of war. You may feel abandoned if yours is the only voice raised in protest at an unjust decision made by a committee. You may feel isolated as you pray fervently for justice and peace alone in your room. But none of us is truly alone. God is with us, hearing our prayers, witnessing our actions. And God unites us with all the other people acting and speaking and praying for justice and peace. There are more of us than you can imagine. We are not alone.

An Invitation to Pray ❧

Look at the activities you anticipate in the weeks to come. Is there something you have already planned that contributes to justice and peace in some way, no matter how small? Is there something you could add to your calendar that might bring a sign of justice or peace to a person or place? Practice making this activity a prayer by turning your intention and attention to God. Recognize how love might motivate your activity. Ask God to guide your speaking and your actions. Open your heart to God's presence in the midst of the activity and express gratitude for the chance to serve with love. Through this practice, you may discover how many opportunities you have to pray with your hands and feet and voices.

CHAPTER FOUR

PRAYING FOR RENEWAL

*Just as speech without silence creates noise, charity
without rest creates suffering.*
—WAYNE MULLER

A wise teaching tale describes the chief devil instruct-
ing the young devils on how to turn people away from God
so as to ensnare them in evil ways. "Don't worry at all about
those people running around doing good and working for
peace and strategizing ways to overcome injustice," the old
devil told them. "I thought they would be the hardest to
tempt and seduce," a young devil replied. "Oh no," the chief
said from experience. "Just watch and wait. Those doing
good will work and give and work and give until they are
worn out. Wait until the light goes out of their eyes. Then
we have them."[1]

Can you identify with this story? I can, for I love to
work! People ask me what I do for fun, and I tell them
I work. I love to be busy getting things done. Nothing is
more satisfying than having a long list of tasks to accomplish
and crossing them off one by one, efficiently and in a timely
manner. I am excited when I am asked to lead one more
retreat, write another article, join with others to plan an
upcoming event for justice and peace. I say yes; I schedule,
I reschedule, I fit in one more thing. And the light begins to
go out of my eyes.

Saying No

There is so much to be done in the struggle for justice and peace. We have the gifts to accomplish great things. People are in need. Someone must speak up. Someone must go. Someone must serve. How can we say no? Yet, according to Thomas Merton, we *must* say no to trying to do too much. "To allow oneself to be carried away by a multitude of conflicting concerns, to surrender to too many demands, to commit oneself to too many projects, to want to help everyone in everything is to succumb to violence. The frenzy of [our] activism neutralizes [our] work for peace. It destroys [our] own inner capacity for peace."[2]

Learning to say no is difficult. In a multitasking world, *not* overworking is countercultural. Our busyness defines our worth; the fullness of our calendars determines our popularity. When we continue to say yes, we feel responsible and important. Yet overwork is likely to turn us into what Parker Palmer, a Quaker author and teacher, calls "functional atheists."[3]

Functional atheists may believe in God, pray to God, express praise and gratitude to God, worship God. But functional atheists behave as if everything depends on them. When we are frantically active, we leave no room for God's guidance, for God's action, for God's grace. Oscar Romero, the Roman Catholic Archbishop of El Salvador who was martyred in 1980, wrote: "We cannot do everything and there is a sense of liberation in realizing that. This enables us to do something, and to do it very well. It may be incomplete, but it is a beginning, a step along the way, an opportunity for God's grace to enter and do the rest."[4]

We must learn to depend on God, recognize our limitations, and honor our need for rest. Times of renewal are holy times, not periods of self-indulgence or selfishness. Sometimes we believe that we should keep on going, that we should not be tired, that resting is a sign of weakness. When we get caught in those ideas, it is wise to turn to the wisdom of Isaiah:

> Even youths will faint and be weary,
> and the young will fall exhausted;
> but those who wait for the Lord
> shall renew their strength,
> they shall mount up with wings like eagles
> they shall run and not be weary,
> they shall walk and not faint (40:30–31).

In the work of justice and peace, we must learn to wait on the Lord. Waiting on the Lord means preparing ourselves to respond prayerfully to God's call. We rest and renew our strength so we will be ready. Praying every day guides us in the waiting and helps us find the patience to wait on the Lord.

Praying Daily

A constant reminder of one's dependence on God is necessary in the lives of many activists. When Gail, a missionary in the Church of the Brethren, went to Nigeria at the age of twenty to teach music to students in thirteen grades from thirty-two countries, she learned that if she went out the door without having had her morning devotions, she was lost. Gail said, "My time in Africa was a crash course in dependence on God." Another woman had a similar experience, although she had lived much of her life without a religious connection. When she traveled to South

Africa to join a community that was actively engaged in the struggle against apartheid, she discovered that it was also grounded in Bible study, prayer, and Holy Communion. She wrote: "I suddenly realized that praying was important for me, that I needed it. Not as a retreat from (dreadful) reality but much more as a time of holding still to face that reality in its horror and beauty, face it as a part of it, but also to experience at the same time that it is not the last word."[5]

As you read of others' practices of daily prayer, you might reflect on your own longing to draw closer to God and renew your soul on a daily basis. What would your prayer look like? What would be right for you? Your form of daily prayer and devotion will depend on your tradition and your need of the moment. Patrick, a college professor who identifies himself as spiritual but not religious, took a group of students to bear witness in Bosnia for five summers. He used a candle as the central image of his daily meditation. He told me that the lighted candle was a reminder of the flame within, a reminder to seek the flame in others, and a reminder to light that flame in places of darkness. "A lit candle loses nothing by lighting another candle," Patrick said.

All these examples of daily prayer—verbal prayer, devotional reading, Bible study, Holy Communion, and the silent lighting of a candle—are shared by people who have served in places of war, poverty, and oppression. If you are serving quietly at home, you can learn from them. You may not face regular hardship and the possibility of death, but each day when you awake, you do not know what will be asked of you and where you will be called to act or speak or bear witness. You may see a disabled person being bullied at a bus stop and feel called to intervene. A friend may call in the middle of your busy day with a story that must be heard. You may pick up the newspaper to read of bombings and destruction and calls for war and retaliation and feel your heart break in sadness. All of us, wherever we serve, need to discover our own way to root ourselves in the love and mercy of God. We must learn to rest, preparing ourselves to respond, as we wait on the Lord.

Part of resting and waiting also includes remembering to pray regularly for ourselves; in our concern for the world, we often forget to include ourselves in our daily prayers. As one young woman wrote: "I have recently learned to pray for myself. I pray that I live and work and speak from pure rather than selfish motives. I pray that I may learn to grow to love others even when I disagree with them. I pray for compassion for myself as I lift myself to God in my anger and unsettledness at the events of the world."[6]

How would you pray for yourself? What is it that you need to sustain and renew you? In a particularly trying time of my own life, I wrote the following prayer. Take it for your own if you wish, or allow it to guide you into finding the words for your own personal prayer. Remember that praying for ourselves opens our hearts to God's grace, renews our spirits, and gives us the courage to continue our work in the world.

> Gracious and merciful God
> I am frightened. Surround me with love
> and ease my fear.
> I am weary. Surround me with stillness
> and bring me rest.
> I am wounded. Surround me with light
> and hasten my healing.
> I am despairing. Surround me with mercy
> and teach me hope.
> Loving God, I open myself to you.

If you have trouble praying alone, community can be helpful in your practice of daily prayer. A woman serving in a halfway house spoke of her joy in praying with her colleagues. Each morning after a staff meeting, all would gather in a circle of love. Prayers were requested and offered. Holy oil was administered to the forehead of each person. They would hold hands as a symbol of their connection as they began their day of ministry and service. "Throughout the day I felt upheld not only by God but by my friends. The daily practice has made an incredible difference in my life," she said.

Suzanne, a Native American activist, also relied on the constant presence of community to sustain her solitary prayer. Although she prayed daily at a home altar she had constructed, she also joined weekly with other native peoples for shared ceremony. In addition to her daily and weekly rituals, she would participate at times of death in wakes for tribal members that would often go on for days. The gatherings alternated between celebration of life and communal mourning. Her attendance at a yearly sweat lodge—a community ritual of purification and prayer—also become an important communal prayer for renewal.[7]

Suzanne's experience of daily, weekly, and yearly prayers and the renewal she found at times of communal mourning remind us that not all prayers of renewal are practiced daily.

Praying During Challenging Times

Preparation for action prayers or action prayers themselves can become part of the rhythm of our prayers for renewal. Cesar Chavez, founder of the farm workers' movement and a practicing Roman Catholic, prepared himself carefully for every action through prayer and fasting.

Whenever his enemies got wind of his preparations, they would exclaim, "Watch out! Cesar Chavez is up to something. He's praying."[8]

While Chavez found his renewal in preparation for action, a young woman found hers in the action itself. After attending a peace march, she said, "I don't want to separate my activism from my prayers for renewal. I am renewed by being present with so many others of like mind and heart. The march became a prayer for me that enabled me to continue working and praying for peace long after I returned home."[9]

Instead of finding renewal within prayerful actions, you may discover that you need another way to pray for renewal when you get discouraged and are wondering whether your work is doing anything to further the cause of justice and peace. Krysso, a young man working to help his community overcome homophobia and heterosexism, turned to music when he felt overwhelmed. Listening to music and making music were his prayers for renewal. One piece that nurtured him was Sally Rogers's song "Love Will Guide Us." The opening line, "Love will guide us, peace has tried us, hope inside us will lead the way,"[10] reminded Krysso to stop looking for hope outside himself, to stop depending on specific signs that his work was making a difference. The song guided him to find hope inside, within the boundaries of his own soul.

Another hopeful song was Si Kahn's "People Like You":

> Old fighter, you sure took it on the chin
> Where'd you ever get the strength to stand
> Never giving up or giving in
> You know I just want to shake your hand

Because
People like you
Help people like me
Go on, go on
People like you
Help people like me
Go on, go on

Old dreamer, with a world in every thought
Where'd you get the vision to keep on
You sure gave back as good as what you got
I hope that when my time is almost gone
        They'll say that
        People like me
        Help people like you
        Go on, go on
        Because people like you
        Help people like me
        Go on, go on
        Go on[11]

These words reminded Krysso that he was not alone in the struggle to end prejudice and oppression and that the songs he was creating would serve to encourage others who were experiencing despair. "When I am singing, it is easier to be hopeful," he said.

In the face of hopelessness and despair, laughter and tears and music can become prayers for renewal. Many activists have told me how laughter helps them regain perspective when they get lost in the struggle and how laughter shared with others builds community. Laughter cannot be commanded or directed, but we can open our hearts to the possibility of delight in unexpected places. We can be willing to seize the funny moment, laugh out loud, and find the humor in our own situations. We can also remember philosopher Alan Watts's pronouncement: "Angels fly because they take themselves so lightly."

Dorothy Day, a founder of the Catholic Worker Movement, was a woman of much good humor and fun. She was also a woman filled with tears. "Like every human being who hungers and thirsts for justice and peace, she too experienced phases of utter exhaustion, sadness and grief. In such times . . . she would withdraw and cry. For long hours, days at a time, she would not eat but just sit and weep."[12] I imagine that her weeping was a prayer of renewal, that her tears released the pain of the struggle and allowed God to console her. Tears that are shed from a broken heart can lead to healing and a resurgence of strength.

Over the years, many people have shared personal and creative prayers to renew themselves in the midst of struggle. One woman involved in AIDS ministry created a "God Box" in which she put a word or an image of something that she needed to turn over to God. This lifted the heaviness of worry that wore her down. Another woman began a "gratitude journal" in which she wrote all that she was grateful for, even in the midst of her active struggle for justice in the workplace. Her list restored her sense of hope, and she returned to her work renewed. A man who was writing about peacemaking would take an hour in the middle of his day to walk in his neighborhood to look for signs of peace that already existed in nature and among people. His prayer reminded him that the peace he longed for already existed and that he was not alone in his desire to create a peaceful world.

As you read these various ways of praying for renewal, have you thought of your own renewal prayers? Have you remembered ways you renew yourself when you are tired, discouraged, or overwhelmed? Do you create something with your hands, write poetry, swim, make music, laugh, or cry? Each of us needs to honor what renews us and create our own prayer forms.

Personal Prayer Forms

To encourage the creation of personal prayers, I asked a group attending a workshop as part of a Peace Colloquy to think of what they did for themselves when they were tired and worn out. "What is your method of self-care?" I asked them. "What do you do to renew yourself in body, mind, and spirit?"

The participants wrote down two or three things they did, and then I asked them to share with one other person. They were hesitant at first, thinking that some of their responses were silly, but after they began they had great fun talking and listening. When we shared methods of self-care in the larger group, there were nods of recognition, occasional laughter, and expressions of surprise. Some of the activities listed were listening to music, baking bread, gardening, washing the car, weaving, making love, taking bubble baths, doing Bible study, going to the zoo, watching cartoons, walking barefoot on the earth, reading mysteries, going to lunch with a friend, singing in a choir, playing tag with children, holding a sleeping cat. The list went on and on.

After all the ideas were shared, I asked them to consider whether they were willing to call these activities prayers for renewal. A shocked silence fell over the room. Somebody murmured, "Washing my car? A prayer?" Another said, "Well, maybe Bible study but not reading mysteries." A lively discussion followed, as I reminded them that with intention and attention, anything could become a prayer. "Well, now that you mention it, I often reflect on God when I am working in the garden," a man said. "There is something awesome in the growth process." "Sometimes when I hold my cat, I imagine that God is holding me," a woman shared. "When I look at the strange and beautiful creatures at the zoo, I know that God has a delightful sense of humor," a man laughed. "Just think of a giraffe!"

We imagined how we could bring our attention to God in the midst of any of these activities and therefore make them prayers. One man, remembering what Mother Teresa had said about how the motivation of love makes any action for justice and peace a prayer, said, "If we engage in these restful and renewing activities motivated by self-love, then they do become prayer. After all, the great commandment says to love our God with all our heart, with all our soul, with all our strength, with all our mind, and our neighbor as ourselves. If we are to act in the world motivated by love, we better begin by loving ourselves."

One way to love ourselves and to show our love for God is to take sabbath time. Sabbath time may be as short as a minute, as when we pause in the midst of an activity and breathe a silent prayer. Sabbath time can be a full year, as in the academic tradition of a sabbatical. Most of us would be wise to find our own sabbath time somewhere between these extremes.

Remember the Sabbath

As we think of remembering the Sabbath in our own lives, we can look to Jewish tradition to guide us. I believe many Christians think of the Sabbath only as a time of solemn quiet and prayer. Solitude and silence before the Lord our God are part of the practice of Sabbath, but so are family and friends, feasting and talking, and play. Sabbath is for communion and intimacy with loved ones as well as with God. Sabbath is about renewing ourselves before God, whose work for justice and peace we are about. It is an opportunity to remember whose world we are struggling to create. And if we hesitate to take time away from our important activities, we might remember that even God rested! "Thus the heavens and the earth were finished, and all their multitude. And on the seventh day God finished the work that he had done, and he rested on the seventh day from all the work that he had done. So God blessed the seventh day and hallowed it, because on it God rested from all the work that he had done in creation" (Genesis 2:1–3).

Because of this creation story, Moses commanded the people of Israel: "Remember the Sabbath day, and keep it holy. Six days you shall labor and do all your work. But the seventh day is a Sabbath to the Lord your God" (Exodus 20:8–10a). In Jesus' time, the law of the Sabbath was honored throughout Israel by observant Jews. When Jesus healed on the Sabbath, he was taken to task by those who opposed him for breaking this holy law. When Jesus was confronted, he said, "Sabbath was made for humankind, not humankind for the Sabbath" (Mark 2:27). Jesus was not disobeying the law so much as he was replacing it with the higher law of love.

It is not easy to remember the Sabbath and keep it holy. For a while one year, I was very faithful in taking sabbath time each week. I would mark a day or part of a day and keep it open and free. Sometimes I would read, or go out into nature, or turn to my journal, or call a friend. I delighted in my sabbath time. But my travel schedule interfered, my workload increased, and the weeks and the months slipped by. "I must return to honoring the Sabbath," I told myself. But much time passed before I found my day. I had it marked; I looked forward to it. I was longing for the open time, a holy time. But when the day came, I was anxious and restless. I didn't know what to do. I could not focus or choose. I could not be still. All I could think of was work. I waited impatiently for the day to end. I learned an important lesson that day. Remembering the Sabbath is a practice. I was out of practice. I was out of touch with myself, out of touch with God. The joy and delight of a holy day had gone out of my life. I had forgotten the Sabbath. The gift of that experience was my grief, for it turned me toward a truth I had denied. The Sabbath was made for me—a gift from a living, loving, merciful God. To receive was to remember. To remember was to receive.

What is your practice of sabbath time? Do you pause in your work for justice and peace to honor God and renew your spirit? Do you think it would be a good idea but don't take the time? When you do create space, do you keep yourself from enjoying it by feeling guilty about not working or doing something "productive?" Our imaginations can give us information about what encourages us and what prevents us from remembering the Sabbath.

A Sabbath Garden

In classes or on retreat with social activists, I often invite the group into an experience of guided imagery to create a sabbath garden. To prepare for this activity, I invite them to close their eyes and relax their bodies by stretching and letting go of tension and settling into their chairs. After a brief period, I suggest that they pay attention to their feelings and thoughts and gently let them go. This opens the heart and mind to the gifts and insights the imagination can provide.

As they relax, participants are invited to create for themselves a beautiful, restful garden. They can put anything in this garden that they wish. Some people create formal English gardens with roses and hedges and precisely placed bushes. Others create wilder gardens with areas of native grasses, meandering streams, and a fallen log to sit on. Some people add animals or birds or a fish pond. Every garden created is unique and provides the individual with an image of a personal place of rest and renewal.

When the participants have created their individual gardens, I guide them into the following exercise: Imagine a wall at one edge of your garden. . . . Slowly approach the wall and examine it closely. . . . It may be of stone or brick or wood. It could be a natural barrier such as a boulder or a stand of trees. . . . In your imagination, find a way to climb the wall, open a gate, or discover some other way to see what is behind the wall. . . . When you have found a way to look into the distance, imagine the world that is calling you to action. . . . See the needs of your families and loved ones. . . . Look closely at your place of work and all that needs to be done. . . . Observe occurrences of injustice, war, and oppression and feel with your heart the needs of suffering people. . . . Experience being pulled toward the never-ending work of justice and peace. . . .

After they have seen the world and feel their hearts moved to do something, I invite them to look back at their sabbath gardens. I ask them to feel the desire for rest and renewal, even as they are aware of the world with all its needs. I then suggest that they remain at the boundary between these two realities, looking back and forth, and to pay attention to their thoughts and feelings. After a brief period, I invite them to turn away from the world, to choose the rest and renewal waiting for them, and to return to the middle of their sabbath garden to reflect on their experience.

To end the exercise, I ask participants to allow the images to begin to fade, to begin to pay attention to the environment of the present moment, to feel their bodies in their chairs, their feet on the floor, to hear the sounds around them. When they are ready, they open their eyes.

A wide variety of responses to this activity are reported. When some people see the world and all its needs, they have a very hard time turning away and returning to the garden. "I felt that I was neglecting my loved ones," a woman said. "I felt ashamed," another woman added, "as if I had turned away from my call to minister to a hurting world." "I couldn't do it," a man confessed. "When you said to return to the garden, I thought 'no way!' and I jumped the wall and went into the world." "I had just the opposite response," an elderly woman said. "I took one look at that hurting world and I fled into the garden, even before you instructed us to." "I felt sad when I returned to the garden," a young man added. "When I was creating the garden I was energized and carefree. I loved being there. But after I saw the world, I could not be as excited about my garden. Life on the other side of the wall had intruded."

Whatever response you have to the guided imagery, it can offer you teachings about your own ability to integrate the Sabbath into your life. We are called to a rhythm of rest and renewal, and we must find time to be in our sabbath gardens, even if it feels uncomfortable. Wayne Muller, the founder of Bread for the Journey, an agency dedicated to issues of world hunger, wrote: "We are a nation of heretic healers, refusing to stop. . . . In our passionate rush to be helpful, we miss things that are sacred, subtle, and important. Doing good requires more than simply knowing what is wrong. Like God in the creation story, we need sabbath time to step back, pause, be quiet enough to recognize what is good."[13] Time in a sabbath garden will allow new visions to emerge and will fill us with faith, hope, and love so we can overflow with the mercy of God.

Overflowing

I have often heard the expression that we are to become channels of God's love. I understand this to mean that we are not supposed to be the source of love, but rather we are to clear and empty ourselves so divine love can come through us. However, if we look at the metaphor closely, it holds us to a constant readiness for God's love to flow through us, with no chance to pause and experience that love for ourselves. I prefer to think that we are called to be reservoirs of God's love, allowing ourselves to be filled and then sharing it with others from our abundance.

When I spoke of this image with a group on retreat, one of the men in attendance said, "I believe Bernard of Clairvaux, twelfth-century theologian, wrote about something similar." After the retreat, he sent me a copy of the saint's words:

> If you are wise . . . you will show yourself a reservoir and not a canal. For a canal pours out as fast as it takes in; but a reservoir waits till it is full before it overflows, and so communicates its surplus. . . . Let the reservoir . . . take pattern from the spring; for the spring does not form a stream or spread into a lake until it is brimful. . . . Be filled thyself then, but discretely, mind, pour out thy fullness. . . . Out of thy fullness help me if thou canst; and if not, spare thyself.[14]

There are any number of ways we can fill our reservoirs. From the many, choose your own way and practice regularly, for without prayers for renewal, our work for justice and peace will be drawn from an empty well and will serve no one. Teacher and pastor Ed Hays wrote: "Works of mercy and justice are to be the overflow of our lives and not the giving of our last drop of energy. Justice and mercy, compassionate service and the pursuit of peace will [naturally] overflow from hearts that pray all ways and always."[15]

An Invitation to Pray

Plan a sabbath time for yourself by setting aside a morning, an afternoon, or a whole day to simply spend time with God. Remember what draws you closer to God and renews your spirit, then make your arrangements ahead of time so you do not spend your sabbath time trying to decide what to do. Do you need a book with you, a journal, paints, music, or a companion? Do you wish to be at home, in nature, or in some other holy space? Begin your sabbath time with a verbal or silent prayer, opening yourself to the grace and the mercy of God. Allow your time to be guided by the spirit as you attend to God in whatever you do. End your sacred time with a prayer of gratitude for whatever you receive. Then look to the future and plan for another opportunity to remember the Sabbath.

CHAPTER FIVE

PRAYING TO BE TRANSFORMED

You can't stand in the midst of the world and struggle for fundamental change unless you are standing in your own space and looking for change within.
—HOWARD THURMAN

When Claire, a young widow with a teenage son, began praying for peace in her family, she wrote the following intercessory prayer and promised herself to pray it every day: "Dear God, please help ease the conflicts that Sam and I have with each other and help us find peace in our home and in our hearts." Although this prayer sounds like an invitation for transformation of Sam, herself, and their relationship, Claire confessed that underneath her words was her own agenda. What she truly wanted was for God to change her son into someone she could live with more easily.

As she prayed her prayer faithfully, she held on to the idea that most of the conflicts at home originated with Sam and that if he would change they would discover the peace she longed for. However, compassion for her son began to creep in around the edges of her prayer, as she recalled all the loss he had experienced in his young life—the death of his father, a change of house and school, and the loss of a best friend.

One day, unable to focus on the words of her prayer, Claire used her imagination and placed Sam and herself in a circle of light. "Suddenly my heart felt cracked open and I began to cry," she said. "I was astounded at the anger and resentment that came up from deep places within me, feelings directed at my late husband for dying and leaving me with a teenage boy to raise alone. I wept for myself as well as for Sam. I wept for the part I had played in the conflict between us. I prayed for forgiveness."

After that experience, Claire continued to pray her prayer for peace in her home and in their hearts, but she opened herself to God's grace and mercy. She began to see Sam in a new light. She discovered ways that she could change her behavior in her interactions with Sam. Claire began her intercessory prayer by asking God to change her son, but she was the one transformed.[1]

We open ourselves to God's transforming love when we pray for justice and peace through intercession, action, or renewal. In surprising ways, our prayers for others work themselves into our own hearts to alter our perceptions, open us to compassion, and sometimes lead us to change our lives. Claire's transformation occurred in the context of intercessory prayer; Matthew, a physician who prayed for justice and peace through an intentional action, experienced transformation in a different way. He believed strongly that abortion was wrong because it did not provide justice for the unborn. He debated joining a prayer vigil outside the home of a doctor who performed abortions, but he chose instead to attend a conference that would use a dialogue format to explore ethical issues surrounding infertility, the use of reproductive technology, and abortion.

To make his participation more intentional and prayerful, Matthew fasted the day before the conference. He arrived at the meeting place early so he could center himself and be fully present to the program. He also prayed for the ability to suspend judgment and to listen with compassion to the others in attendance. During the course of the day, he listened to many stories and heard a wide range of opinions. The participants were respectful of differences and freely shared ideas and many personal experiences. As he listened, he began to wonder whether the abortion issue might be better argued in the hearts and minds of individuals rather than in the courts.

Weeks after the conference, Matthew wrote me a letter sharing his experience:

> My action prayer has prompted me to reflect on the following: the stewardship of the gift of life; the difference between what is legal and what is moral; the fact that we don't know as much about other people's reality as we think we do; what it means that God knew us in our mother's womb. The dialogue at the conference reminded me of the reassuring truth that God stands with us in all our hard decisions and that God's grace is sufficient for every circumstance. My intentional and purposeful attendance at the conference was a prayer of openness, acceptance, empathy and understanding. I will still work for justice for the unborn, but I will do it with a changed heart, for the conference brought me closer to God and closer to my sisters and brothers by helping me see the struggles of others as God sees them.

Claire was transformed through her practice of intercessory prayer, while Matthew received God's grace through his prayerful action. Agnes, an administrative secretary with a secure job and a home in the suburbs, was transformed while attending to her prayers for renewal. "I had gone to a midnight mass to renew my energy and restore a sense of balance in my life," she said. "As I knelt in prayer, I reflected on the scripture reading from the gospel of

Matthew: 'Foxes have holes, and the birds of the air have nests; but the Son of Man has nowhere to lay his head' (Matthew 8:20). I suddenly realized that the homelessness experienced by many in our city was the homelessness of Jesus."

In the following weeks, as she prayed about the connection she had made between Jesus and homelessness, Agnes saw the relevance for her own life. Although she had never been physically homeless, she had experienced for many years a restlessness—an experience she called "homelessness of my heart." A feeling of solidarity began to grow in relation to the homeless people of the city. She understood that she was being called from her spiritual homelessness to live among them. Agnes left her home and her work and moved into a religious community of lay people to become a cook for the Catholic Worker.[2]

Although transformation of our hearts and lives can occur through any form of prayer, we can also be intentional in our prayers for transformation. We can pray for our lives to be changed, just as we long for the world to be changed, and seek inner transformation with as much fervor as we seek to create a world of justice and peace. In other words, we can be willing to become the change we wish to see in the world.[3]

Looking Deep Within

Intentional prayers for transformation are not easy, for they require us to examine our minds and hearts and souls for the seeds of prejudice, oppression, and violence deep within. To encourage this prayerful self-examination in a group of people who had gathered to learn about working and praying for justice, I asked the participants to create a collective list of the reasons we have injustice in the world.

The list they generated included greed, territorial pursuits, lack of compassion, prejudice, quest for power, no forgiveness, ignorance, desperation, poverty, self-righteousness. When they had finished, I asked them to look over the list and to choose the one thing they thought caused the greatest suffering in the world.

When they each had made their selection, they wrote their chosen word at the top of a piece of paper. I then led them in a brief centering exercise to prepare them to prayerfully respond to the following questions:

Where do you see this reason for injustice and oppression in the world?
Where do you see it in your nation?
Where do you see it in your city?
In your community?
In your congregation?
In your family?
Where do you see it in your heart?

As the questions moved closer to home, the room got more and more quiet. They had begun to realize that what they believed to be the source of the most suffering in the world resided in their personal lives and in their own hearts.

In the sharing after the exercise, one man said, "I chose 'ignorance.' It was easy to see it in the nation and the city and my community. When I got to my church, I could see it, but I didn't like to admit it. Then my family and myself . . . it's hard, but it is there too. I also realized I am guilty of self-righteousness as well, for that was my feeling at the beginning of this exercise when I was seeing ignorance only 'out there.'"

Another participant said, "I picked greed partly because I take such pride in my own generosity and I am very judgmental of people who hoard their resources. As I moved closer and closer to my own heart, I realized that I may be generous with my money but I am greedy for experience. I want more travel, more adventures, more people in my life. I may be generous, but I am also greedy."

These two people from the group were beginning the process of prayerful self-examination and recognizing the roots of suffering in their own hearts. They also uncovered some opposite qualities residing within themselves. The woman realized she was generous and greedy. The man owned his ignorance, but his wisdom helped him see his self-righteousness. So, in fact, he was both ignorant and wise.

If you were to do this exercise, what would you discover? What factors that contribute to oppression and injustice reside in your own heart? What contradictions do you live with? As you begin to look within yourself, remember that the purpose of such self-examination is not to chastise yourself or blame yourself for the problems of the world. The purpose of prayerful self-reflection is to bear witness to yourself, to be with yourself exactly as you are. It will not be easy to see some of your hidden qualities without rushing to fix them, erase them, or deny them. But if you can see all your qualities with a beginner's mind, with no preconceived ideas of how you should be, you will open yourself to God's grace and mercy. You will allow and welcome God's healing power to be about the mystery of transformation, healing even the violence that lies deep within.

Finding Seeds of Violence

One of the most difficult contradictions for us to acknowledge is the violence we carry in our own hearts, even as we long for and work for peace. Who among us has not felt the urge to strike out at one who has hurt us, to hurl cruel words at people we dislike, to take revenge on those who have done us wrong? If we are honest with ourselves, we know that the possibility of violence lies within. This violence is not the feeling of anger we hold against one who has hurt us, for anger is a human and holy response to injustice and evil. But when we experience anger, we must avoid what theologian Reinhold Neibuhr understood to be anger's two temptations—hatred and vengeance.[4] If we are to take Neibuhr's warning seriously, we need to reflect on how hatred and the desire for revenge are present in our own lives.

We don't like to think of ourselves as people who hate, but the word slips off our tongue with ease. Sometimes we use it in regard to our personal preferences: "I hate lima beans." "I just hate standing in line." "Don't you hate growing old?" Sometimes the word *hate* is directed at another person: "I hate you, I hate you, I hate you!" one child might scream at another after being called an ugly name. "I hate the neighbor who abused me," a young adult might whisper after revealing an incident of childhood assault. Sometimes hate escalates into violence. People who hated homosexuals, first in thought, then in words, and finally with action, tied the young gay college student Matthew Sheppard to a fence in Wyoming, beat him unconscious, and left him to die.

To avoid the temptation to hate, we can learn to feel the anger that belongs with the experience of injustice and evil and find other ways to express it. We might simply begin watching our language and stop using the word *hate* in response to any situation. A far more difficult practice is to experience our anger and allow it to motivate us to speak and act prophetically. We can learn to speak loudly and clearly against cruelty and oppression and with compassion for those in unjust situations. We can discover actions that lead to reconciliation rather than retaliation. Prophetic words and actions keep us connected to God, whereas hate separates us from the heart of God. Civil rights activist Fanny Lou Hamer expressed the effects of hate this way: "I feel sorry," she said, "for anybody that could let hate wrap them up. Ain't no such thing as I can hate anybody and hope to see God's face."[5]

Revenge is another temptation in response to anger about injustice and oppression. If we experience the desire to retaliate against those who have wronged us or others, Saint Paul's words in his letter to the Christian community in Rome may remind us where revenge belongs. He wrote: "Vengeance is mine said the Lord" (Romans 12:19). Before Paul, the Hebrew people understood that vengeance belonged to God, but they did not hesitate to tell God exactly how that revenge should be enacted. This portion of Psalm 58 (6–8) gives God clear instructions:

> O God, break the teeth in their mouths,
> tear out the fangs of the young lions, O Lord!
> Let them vanish like water that runs away;
> like grass let them be trodden down and wither.
> Let them be like the snail that dissolves into slime;
> like the untimely birth that never sees the sun.

When we use the Psalms as a guide and pray our desire for revenge, we turn our deepest and most destructive thoughts over to God and trust that God will ultimately vindicate the just in God's own time. Shouting, yelling, crying our instructions to God can release our anger and give our desire for revenge to God. When our instructions for vengeance are fierce, graphic, and specific, they free us from the need for personal revenge. It may seem wrong to express such rage to God, but when we speak the unspeakable in prayer, we are released from the need to act. Facing our temptations to hate and seek revenge and giving them to God make us available to God's healing grace, as a social activist named Marie discovered during Holy Communion.

Marie was moved to pray for her own transformation after recognizing the possibility of violence in her own heart. With the Eucharist disintegrating into her own body, she prayed for the promised transformation within. Later, Marie put her private prayer into words.

Lord, transform my anger and my fear.
Help me to journey to the center of myself
and find the courage to face my shadow.
I know that when I deny and repress my shadow
I project onto others
and become violent against them.
Lord, through the body and blood of Your Son,
may the potential seed of violence that resides in me
be transformed into love.
May the seeds of violence that germinate
in our world be healed and transformed
through love, into love. Amen[6]

When we are willing to bear witness to ourselves and acknowledge the seeds of violence within, it is important not to condemn and punish ourselves for our thoughts and feelings, for if we do, we continue the cycle of violence. Instead, it is time to confess to God what we have discovered and pray for forgiveness. But first we must learn to forgive others.

Forgiving and Forgiven

"Forgive us our sins as we forgive those who sin against us," says one version of the Lord's Prayer. Note the order of these familiar words. They indicate that if we are to know God's forgiveness, we first need to offer our forgiveness to others. However, forgiving is not easy. It is not something we can one day decide to do and then simply do it. Forgiveness is a much more complex process. Have you ever forgiven another and then later realized that you were still angry and still had fantasies of revenge, and that when you thought of that person it was always with resentment? This doesn't mean that your forgiveness wasn't sincere; it simply means that you had only taken one step in the long, slow process of forgiveness. Jesus indicated the slowness of the process when he responded to Peter's question as to whether seven were enough times to forgive his brother or sister. Jesus said, "I do not say seven times, but seventy times seven" (Matthew 18:22).

However long the process may take, we are called to practice forgiveness in issues small and large. Are you willing to forgive a friend who has kept you waiting over half an hour? Are you willing to forgive the children who frightened your son so badly that he ran home in tears? Am I willing to forgive the college professor who ridiculed me in front of my classmates? Am I willing to forgive those who judged me for my decision to divorce?

Marietta Jaeger was faced with one of the most difficult issues of forgiveness that any of us could imagine when her daughter was murdered. She wrote about the need for forgiveness from her own experience and experiences of other families whose loved ones had died violently: "Victim families have every right initially to the normal, valid, human response of rage, but those persons who retain a vindictive mindset ultimately give the offender another victim. Embittered, tormented, enslaved by the past, their quality of life is diminished. However justified, our unforgiveness undoes us."[7]

EMBRACING THE WORLD

If we take Jaeger's words seriously, forgiving someone is less about the other person and more about our own hearts. Forgiving someone else, even the person who has sinned most grievously against us, liberates us from a prison of rage and our attachment to revenge. How do we begin the long, complex process of forgiveness? We start where our hearts are and take all our thoughts and feelings to God in prayer. We might begin our prayer with "God, I want to forgive but do not know how." Or even, "I don't want to forgive, God; I'm too angry and sad. Help me!"

Trying to forgive another without God's help is very difficult. We need God to guide us through the complicated steps of growing in forgiveness. This is particularly true when the one who has hurt us is not sorry and expresses no remorse. But even then, if we recognize our enslavement to the past and pray for the courage to forgive, God will soften our hearts and transform our thinking so that we will ultimately be able to say, "I forgive you." Finding the strength to say those words and being freed from the torment of unforgiveness is a gift from God. To receive this gift, we may need to turn to God over and over and over again.

When we have experienced God's gift, have learned to forgive others, and then begin to practice the art of forgiveness in our daily lives, we are ready to receive God's forgiveness for the violence, oppression, greed, or prejudices in our own hearts and the hurtful behaviors we have done to others. We are ready to truly pray, "Forgive us our sins as we forgive those who have sinned against us." Sometimes we can go to the person we have wronged, ask for forgiveness, and be forgiven. When we are not forgiven, and even if we are, we may still need to take our wrongs into prayer and open ourselves to receive God's forgiveness. Yet receiving

God's forgiveness and then forgiving ourselves is often more difficult than forgiving another.

A colleague of mine recognized how hard it was to receive forgiveness as he continued to berate himself for having betrayed a friend years before. His friend had filed a sexual harassment complaint at work and was having great difficulty with the lengthy legal process. She felt isolated and victimized in her struggle for justice and turned to her friend for support. He soon tired of the ongoing saga and began making excuses not to see her and then stopped returning her phone calls. Months later, he learned through a mutual friend that she had lost the case, been fired from her job, and moved away. He wanted to contact her but was unable to discover where she had gone. He was unable to make amends.

Years later, during Holy Week he heard the familiar story of Peter's betrayal of Jesus (Mark 14:66–72). Peter told Jesus he would never deny him, and then Peter did—three times. After Peter's final denial, he remembered Jesus foretelling the betrayal, and he broke down and wept. Upon hearing these words from scripture, my colleague realized he had never wept tears of confession that would allow him to receive forgiveness. He had held his sin close and not offered it to God. Freed by the biblical words and the image of Peter weeping, he began to cry. "The tears have set me free," he said. "I have spent many years in regret, chastising myself, reminding myself what a terrible thing I had done, unable to ask her forgiveness. My tears are beginning to free me, they are a new and different form of prayer."

Forgiveness can be discovered through our tears shed in the presence of God. When we weep for ourselves and the hurt we have caused, when we cry out from the pain of what we have done, we are reaching out to God in prayer. Our tears open our hearts to receive the forgiveness that

God so freely offers, and with this grace we can begin to forgive ourselves.

Looking deeply within by examining our hearts for seeds of violence and by looking honestly at our behavior in regard to others is not only for individuals but for groups as well—congregations, corporate bodies, nations. For justice to be done and peace to be made, all parties need to take responsibility for their attitudes and behaviors that have led to oppression, conflict, or war. Seeing the truth in our own culpability, confessing our sins to God, opening ourselves to receive God's gracious forgiveness makes us ready to participate fully in the reign of God. But transformation is not a one-time event for groups any more than it is for individuals. Collectively, we may need to practice forgiving others, confessing our sins, and praying for forgiveness seven times seventy times.

From Words to Silence

Forgiving others through God's mercy, confessing our sins, and seeking forgiveness from others and from God are prayers of the *kataphatic* tradition—a Greek word meaning "full of content." Kataphatic prayers use words and images, music and song, actions with hands and feet and voices. Prayers of intercession, supplication, praise, confession, gratitude, thanksgiving, and renewal, whether spoken, written, sung, drawn, danced, or imagined, are all kataphatic prayers. They are the most commonly used prayers of our traditions.

There is another way to pray—the apophatic way, which is described by the mystical paths of the world's religions. *Apophatic* is a Greek word meaning empty, without content. Apophatic prayer uses no words or images, asking for nothing, desiring nothing, expecting nothing, receiving nothing. This form of prayer does not give something to God, as when we offer praise, instructions, or glory. It asks nothing of God, as in intercession, supplication, or confession. Rather, apophatic prayer is a receptive form of prayer in which we empty ourselves and silently open our very souls to whatever God has to offer.

But how do we become empty of all questions, thoughts, feelings, goals, and desires, with nothing to say and nothing to ask? How do we exist without our thoughts? Travel if there is nowhere to go? Empty ourselves into emptiness? How do we do something that cannot be done? Become someone we already are? These are mystical questions that have no logical answers. In the rational world we find them paradoxical and confusing. Why entertain questions with no answers or pursue something that has no clear way and no destination? Why open ourselves to experiences that cannot be defined, measured, or counted upon? Mystics of all traditions would answer us from their lived experience and assure us that the apophatic way transforms hearts and lives and makes possible the gift of contemplation.

Contemplation is a more familiar term that parallels the apophatic way. Mystics describe contemplation as something we receive rather than something we do. German mystic Meister Eckhart wrote, "God does not ask anything else of you except that you let yourself go and let God be God in you."[8] We can practice this "letting go into God" through contemplative prayer—a form of prayer that points us toward the apophatic way and allows God to be God in us and opens us to receive the grace of contemplation.

A popular form of contemplative prayer is centering prayer, made accessible to those who work and pray for justice and peace through the extensive writings of Father Thomas Keating.[9] In the practice of centering prayer, you simply consent to God's call to relationship. You offer an affirmative response to this holy invitation by sitting quietly for twenty minutes, simply being in the presence of God. But your intention to be with God and your attention on God will most likely be interrupted by distracting thoughts. You will forget about God and turn your attention to whatever intrigues your body, feelings, or mind. You might be distracted by your hunger or your fatigue, your gratitude or your grief, a letter you need to write or an idea for a new painting. As thoughts appear, you will probably follow these distractions with more thoughts, as when the experience of hunger makes you remember when you last ate or starts you thinking about what you want for dinner. This could lead to concern about your health or your weight and cause you to remember what the doctor said at your last check-up. Then you could begin to wonder about other health concerns . . . and then you have wandered far from your intention to spend time with God while your attention has been elsewhere.

Whenever distractions occur, notice that you have been absent from God and use a prayer word (sometimes called a sacred word) to bring your attention back to God. A prayer word is any word you select to remind yourself of your intention to spend time with God. The word could be *God, Jesus, love, spirit, mercy, rest, grace*—anything that will draw you gently back into God's presence. If you prefer, you could use an image such as a flame, a dove, a tree, or a well. Take your time selecting your word or image, and when you have chosen one, stay with it. Otherwise, you can distract yourself during centering prayer by thinking about whether you have decided wisely or what other word might be better than yours. You might even spend all your prayer time wandering away from God in pursuit of the perfect sacred word or image!

Your prayer word is not to be used as a mantra, which is a word or phrase repeated continually during meditation time. A prayer word or image is only invoked when you realize your attention has wondered away from the presence of God. Your wandering attention is to be expected, for it is human nature to think and feel. Do not judge your thoughts or try to banish them. Honor your thoughts and let them go, and when you get caught by them and they lead you away, notice you are no longer attending to God but to something else. Silently say the prayer word to bring yourself back to your original intention: God.

When I sit in centering prayer, I begin by relaxing my body and attending to my breathing to honor my body in this process of prayer. I say a simple intention: "This time is to be with You." Usually, I have a moment of delight and relief that I am resting in the presence of God. As I sink into the experience, my mind and heart drift away from God to another concern. I realize that the chair is uncomfortable and I think of changing positions. Or I hear the neighbor's dog barking and I am annoyed at the sound. I begin to imagine complaining so that the dog will not bother me. The conversation takes form in my mind—and then I catch myself. I have wandered away from God. I say my prayer word and I am back in the presence of God, only to be gone again a few moments later. This time I disappear into my plans for the day. I begin to worry about a meeting that is scheduled—oops. I'm gone again. I say my prayer word and return to the presence of God. This pattern of attending to God, slipping away, attending to where I am, and gently returning to God usually continues for my full twenty minutes of prayer. This is not a judgment of my prayer time; it is simply a fact.

Judging ourselves or our prayer time is not helpful. I could admonish myself for having to use the prayer word a hundred times during my twenty minutes. I could congratulate myself for not having been distracted at all. But when I place the worth of the time on my failure or success, I put myself at the center of the prayer rather than God. Centering prayer is not about doing it right or well or easily. When we sit down to spend our time with God, there is no way to do centering prayer wrong, even if we are distracted one thousand times in twenty minutes. As Father Thomas once said, "The only way to fail at centering prayer is to not show up."

When we show up faithfully, we may begin to notice subtle changes in our lives. We may discover that we are more awake to the world around us, growing in compassion or discovering wisdom. These changes are the fruits of prayer. However, they are not the goals of prayer. We do not practice contemplative prayer to become holy. We practice simply to be with God, love God, and allow God to do the work of transformation in our hearts and souls. Usually we are unable to experience this transformation immediately. Our lives are just as they have always been and our hearts may remain heavy or filled with anxiety. When that happens, it is easy to think that the prayer "isn't working," but we need to remember that this prayer is about surrendering to God and being willing to let God transform us in God's own time. Centering prayer, as well as any other form of contemplative prayer, is about suspending expectations and surrendering into the mystery and the oneness of God.

Union with God

Contemplative prayer can, with God's grace, draw us into union with God where we are lost in God and God is lost in us. Although still separate (we do not *become* God), our intimacy is so deep that we are able to know as God knows, see as God sees, hear as God hears, and love as God loves.

This mystical union transforms us and graces us, not with a new image of God but with a new relationship to the world. Contrary to the mistaken belief that mystical experiences draw people out of the world to focus on the interior life, true mysticism draws us into the world, liberated to engage life more fully and work more lovingly for justice and peace.[10]

Liberated and transformed, we see the world and others with the eyes of God, hear with the ears of God, and feel with the heart of God. We know that we are related to all people, all creatures, and all of creation so that like St. Francis of Assisi we can call the sun our brother and the moon our sister. Freed from old ways of seeing the world and people as separate, foreign, or "other," we experience everything as part of ourselves and God. Our union with God transforms our attitudes, speech, and actions so that we live more gracefully, not only working for justice but living justly, not only making peace but being peace.

Does union with God, mystical experience, oneness with all of creation seem beyond you? Do you wonder about the reality of things beyond your rational understanding? Most of us do question what we have not seen. Yet haven't you glimpsed the mystical world or had your own mystical moment? What of the time you knew exactly what you needed to do, even though everyone else believed differently? Remember how you looked into the eyes of an animal in the wild and felt a kinship. Have you ever stood on a street in a strange city and had someone greet you as a friend or read of a tragedy in another's life and felt as if your own heart were breaking?

These mystical moments help us know the reality of God's healing and transformative love in our lives. As we pray to be transformed, we may be healed and changed in ways we cannot imagine—healed and changed not for our

EMBRACING THE WORLD

own sake but for the sake of the world. If my need for power and control is softened by God's healing grace, I will not need to convince others that my way is right and will become more accepting of differences. If your need for affection and esteem is met by experiencing God's unconditional love, you will be more loving to others and less interested in receiving love for yourself. As each of us opens our hearts to the possibility of union with God and all creation, a healing force is released, bringing with it the experience and knowledge that truly we are one. In the playful words of the Sufi poet Rumi, we would know that

> To meet my thousand thousand faces
> I roam the world;
> The dirtiest grass
> Wears the sunlight of my skin:
> I stand in this stream, myself, and laugh.[11]

An Invitation to Pray

Think of someone in your life you need to forgive, someone who has hurt you or a loved one physically, emotionally, or spiritually. Or ask yourself if there is something you need to be forgiven for. In either case, you may be at the beginning of the forgiveness process or you may already be engaged in forgiving another or yourself. Take your desire to forgive to God, speaking from your heart, asking for help, sharing all you feel. You may wish to turn to the Psalms, write, draw, or dance your prayer, or sit silently, opening yourself to God's mercy. However you pray, remember that the liberation you experience and the peace you gradually discover in your heart through forgiveness will bring freedom and peace to others. Your prayers are one step toward healing a broken world.

CHAPTER SIX

PRAYING FOR DISCERNMENT

*If we are listening for the will of God, it behooves us to
listen with our hearts, the marrow of our bones, and
our whole skin, as well as with our ears.*
—PATRICIA LORING

Recently divorced and soon to be eligible for early
retirement, David was trying to decide what to do with the
rest of his life. He felt as if he were being faced with a real
choice for the first time. "In the past, I chose what was in
front of me or what was expected of me," he said. "In high
school, I chose to run track because it was my father's sport.
I went to college at my mother's alma mater. I married the
woman I met in my first year of teaching. When we discovered we were unable to have children, my wife did not want
to adopt, so I am not a father. Then a year ago she moved
out, and our divorce was final last month."

A man of deep faith, David believed that the situation
he was in, as painful as it was, could be an opportunity for
him to discern how God wanted him to live and what God
wanted him to do. "Everyone I know has advice for me,"
he said. "They tell me to take a trip around the world, start
dating and get married, go back to school, move to Mexico,
take up a new hobby, start running again. But I don't want
to do what others tell me. I want to listen to God and be
guided in my choices. I think I want to be of service to others, but above all, I want to be faithful."

Two key words in David's statement are *listen* and
faithful, for faithful listening is at the heart of discernment.

When we pray for discernment, we are asking for guidance about the choices we have before us. We are seeking God's counsel about how we are to live our lives. If we are to hear what God has to offer, we must enter into receptive prayer ready to listen. We have already witnessed some listening prayers in the stories told in the previous chapters. Lois, the student who prayed for Osama Bin Laden, did not sit down to decide what or who to pray for. She listened, and the need to pray for him came from deep within. Sala Nolan listened to the call of spirit and went to Oklahoma to protest the death penalty. While serving in Africa, Gail knew to pray each day before she left the house. Her decision came from listening to the needs of her heart. My colleague who had betrayed his friend listened to the words of scripture and recognized himself. He wept his confession and experienced forgiveness.

What were these people listening for? What did they hear? Did they receive answers to questions? Did they even know they were praying for discernment? These and similar questions arise in any discussion of discernment, for we want to know what discernment is, how to ask for guidance, and ways to hear the answers. Yet when we pray for discernment, we are expressing our willingness to engage in a life process of listening for God's desire for our lives. There is no set prayer, no outline of the process, no formula for assurance. There is only the willingness to listen with all of who we are.

Before I came to that conclusion, I thought that discernment was problem solving with a spiritual dimension. I believed we were simply to include God in the process of rational decision making. We could consult others and gather as much information as possible, and then we might offer a prayer for clarity. Or we could list everything in favor of one possibility and list everything against it, and then pray for guidance. Or we could imagine the outcome and consequences of each action and then seek God's wisdom. Or, with everything before us, as we weighed the pros and cons to make a logical choice, we could pray for affirmation of our decision, for encouragement to proceed, or for a pleasing outcome. After much reflection, I began to realize that this understanding of discernment makes God an assistant in a rational decision-making process, instead of God being at the heart of a decision where we engage the mind and feelings to help pay attention to the possibilities and choices before us. With God in the center of discernment, we surrender into not knowing before we know.

We may feel frustrated at not being able to outline the process of discernment, render an exact definition, or really understand what "surrender into not knowing" means. However, descriptions of the experience of discernment and poetic images of discernment can help us learn to pray for discernment.

Experiences and Images of Discernment

Betty Schwicker came to speak at my home church about her experience on mission in the Middle East and shared with us her process of discernment that led her there. Betty is a retired social worker whose pastor told her about a job that had opened at the YMCA in Palestine. He thought she was perfect for the position and urged her to apply. Betty knew she needed to pray for discernment. Was God truly calling her to the mission field? Was she avoiding something by going? Did she have the gifts and graces to be present to people overwhelmed by war? She was afraid, felt inadequate, and wondered how she would cope in a foreign land so far away from home. Betty told me she felt as Peter must have felt when he heard Jesus say, "Very truly, I tell you, when you were younger, you used to fasten your own belt and to go wherever you wished. But when you grow old, you will stretch out your hands, and someone else will fasten a belt around you and take you where you do not wish to go" (John 21:18).

Betty's lack of clarity remained with her, even as she requested information about the position, filled out the application, and began to look at the possibility of bringing the present chapter of her life to a close. She was not sure she would really go, even when she accepted the job offer, informed her family, and began to put her things in storage. Betty had surrendered into not knowing, into mystery. "I was still ambivalent when I went to the missionary commissioning service, which was to make me an official emissary from my church," she said. "The ceremonies began, and I was so confused I had to leave the room. Could I really do this unexpected thing? I prayed for guidance. And what I discovered was that I had thought that this choice was mine. It really wasn't. God had actually made this decision for me long ago. God knew when I didn't."

By staying with the mystery, Betty was able to "apprehend" rather than "comprehend" her decision.[1] To apprehend means to perceive or become aware of something and to recognize its meaning. To comprehend means to know something or to understand what is happening. The difference between the two is subtle. *Apprehending* is more like catching sight of a butterfly and recognizing the meaning it has for you as you watch it flit by; *comprehending* is more like trying to understand the flight or the path of the butterfly. Both ways of perception may include wonder and gratitude, and neither way alters the presence or the flight of the butterfly. Like the butterfly, the desire of God for our lives is constant. In discernment, we wait to see it rather than try to figure it out.

As Betty prepared to go to Palestine, she proceeded in her actions, even as she waited for a glimpse of God's hope for her. She did not dismiss her rational mind, but she did not stifle the process by the need to understand. In staying open in her discernment process, Betty became aware of God's role in her decision and grasped the meaning of her actions.

Apprehending rather than comprehending is only one way to describe the experience of discernment. Catholic writer Paul Wilkes describes the process in another way. He writes that discernment is "a growing light, a growing awareness, a confidence in both God and ourselves. Not so much a series of peak experiences, it is more a background presence."[2] I witnessed this growing awareness and confidence in a woman wrestling with her decision of whether to leave her religious order after twenty-two years. She met with me weekly and told me stories about her early years, her decision to enter the religious life at twenty-three, how the sisters of the community had welcomed her and given her a spiritual as well as a physical home. She talked about the blessings and the trials of religious life, the gifts she had received, and the opportunities she had sacrificed. After months of storytelling, she arrived at my office one day to tell me calmly that she had decided to leave. "I don't know why or exactly where I am going," she said, "but God will be with me. I won't be alone." There was no blinding insight, no peak experience. She simply knew what she had to do and was confident that God would bless her choice.

A more poetic description of discernment is offered by Wendy Wright, a writer in the field of contemporary spirituality. She imagines discernment as the "turning of the sunflower to the sun . . . or the restless seeking of a heart longing to find its way home to an estranged lover." She goes on to say that "discernment is about feeling texture, assessing weight, watching the plumb line, listening for overtones, searching for shards, feeling the quickening, surrendering to love. It is being grasped in the Spirit's arms and led in the rhythms of an unknown dance."[3]

This series of images invites our reflection on our own experiences of discernment. When have you been in the process of making a life decision and slowly, almost imperceptibly, found yourself turning toward one particular option? Have you ever made a choice based on the energy you felt as you thought about one possibility, a quickening of your soul when you imagined moving in that direction? Have you ever surrendered to love or been grasped in the Spirit's arms to dance an unfamiliar rhythm?

Jennifer, a young seminary student, realized she was having trouble with discernment because she was living with her back to God, closed to the possibility of being grasped in the Spirit's arms. If the invitation to dance had arrived, she wouldn't have known it. "I spent all of last year saying that God was not speaking to me and that God would not tell me what to do with my life. The reality was that I had my back to God. Now that I have turned around, God has the chance to communicate with me. And if God chooses not to 'speak,' I will still be waiting with my heart open and with my face turned toward God's loving presence."[4]

Waiting with our hearts open is necessary as we pray for justice and peace, for then our work and our prayers will be a response to God's promptings rather than motivated by our own idea of what needs to be done. When we listen to God and the movement of the Spirit, we will discover where, when, and how we are to serve, and we will know whether it is time to act or time to be still. God's love for us and the world will guide us in our decisions about renewal and reveal to us how our own hearts need healing.

Opening our hearts and listening for guidance are the ways of discernment, and stories and images are helpful in getting a picture of discernment. But they still do not tell us exactly how to pray for discernment. This is because there are no steps and no formulas; discernment is more a readiness of heart than any method of prayer. There are, however, qualities or attitudes that we can develop to make our lives more discerning—that turn us like sunflowers to the sun.

Trusting God

First and foremost, discernment depends on our faith and trust in a God who is with us—not God as an abstraction, distant, and remote but God with us, guiding us, sustaining us, enfolding us, loving us, and working actively for a just and peaceful world. This knowledge of and faith in God comes from our lived experience.

You might pause for a moment and remember a time when you experienced God with you. Don't search for blinding revelations or a thundering voice, but like Elijah, who heard the Lord in a still small voice, search for the presence of God in your life by remembering whispers, promptings, and longings. Remember a time when you felt held by love or a time when you turned in an unexpected direction to find something you didn't even know you were looking for. Remember a longing that prompted you to take a risky step into the unknown or a time walking in the woods when all your senses let you know God was with you.

When I look for those moments, I remember an experience when I was in my early forties. My life was fairly settled; I had work I loved, many friends, and opportunities for travel and adventure. I was studying transpersonal psychology and practicing Zen meditation. Then I got the strange idea to go to seminary. "I'm not even sure I'm a Christian," I said to myself and dismissed the possibility. But the nudging wouldn't go away, so I began to explore the options. Soon I was auditing a class, then applying for admission, thinking all along that going to seminary was not logical and was a bad idea. When I was admitted and began my studies, people asked me why I had come to seminary. I could only respond that I really didn't know; I only knew that I couldn't *not* come.

In a very different way, a dear friend of mine felt God's presence when her grandson died. She turned to her practice of centering prayer and immediately fell into the merciful arms of God. "I felt held," she said, "and I knew my beloved grandson was in the heart of God." Her grief was fierce, but she did not drown in it, for God was with her in her weeping and in the long process of healing.

Having faith in the presence of God grows from remembering these experiences. Sometimes we do not recognize God in the moment, as in my case. I was not sure that God was sending me to seminary. Only in retrospect did I come to believe with confidence that my longings and the promptings I received were of God. I saw no other explanation for my action. Like Peter, I had been led where I did not wish to go. My friend, on the other hand, knew God's presence in the moment. She had no question that her comfort and solace came from God. Look to your history, look in the moment, and discover where God has been and is with you. In this way, you can deepen your faith and trust in a loving and immediate God.

Giving Up Control

Another quality for becoming discerning is the willingness to give up control and become receptive and open to guidance. Receptivity is not the same as passivity when we give away all power and responsibility and simply allow to happen whatever may. Instead, when we are receptive we actively bring all of who we are to the listening process. We listen attentively for the gift of discernment that comes from God. When we speak of discernment as a gift, we make it a noun rather than a verb.[5]

Usually the word *discern* is a verb, with ourselves as the subject. "I need to discern my call to ministry." "I want to discern the next step in my journey." "As a community, we need to discern our vision and our plan of action." When *discernment* is a verb, we have a project to do with an outcome to accomplish. However, if it is a noun, *discernment* becomes a gift that we receive. Praying for discernment becomes a stance in life, a way of being, a readiness of heart that calls us to live with all senses awake, heart open, and hands unclenched ready to receive. Living our prayers of discernment calls us to humility.

Discovering Humility

Humility does not come from being humiliated by others or from focus on our faults, wounds, and sins. True humility develops as we draw closer to God, for God's greatness illuminates our smallness, and in God's wholeness we sense our incompleteness. Recognizing our smallness and our dependence on God, we are open to guidance. As the Psalmist wrote, God "leads the humble in what is right, and teaches the humble his way" (Psalm 25:9). Humility is necessary for discernment because to be humble in heart means that we will recognize the limits of our own knowledge and turn to God for guidance.[6]

Discovering humility was the key for a young priest torn between two opportunities for ministry. One was to serve as a missionary in Southeast Asia, and the other was to pursue his education in order to prepare him for seminary teaching. Both were appealing to him, and both of them seemed to be of God. He agonized over his decision. He would move toward one option and then pull back. He would make lists of reasons to accept the other option and then second guess himself and end up more confused. He had in his mind that he ought to be able to figure out which path to take. Then his spiritual director pointed out the arrogance of his thinking and encouraged him to approach the dilemma with humility. Putting aside his need to control his ministry, he asked God for guidance. He entered into a silent listening prayer every day. But nothing came clear; no answer solved his problem; he still did not know what to do. He became frustrated and anxious but he continued to pray. Then early one morning, he received what he did not expect. His anxiety had lifted, and he received the gift of peace. He became comfortable with not knowing and was willing to wait for the direction to be made clear. He realized that through humility he had surrendered to the mystery and the mercy of God.

Becoming Still

The only way we can listen and surrender is by becoming still—a fourth condition for discernment. The gift the priest received in his process of discernment was stillness and the willingness to be patient and not force an answer. Gandhi was well known for his ability to be still and wait. The story is told that when Gandhi was asked by Indian leaders what to do about the British salt tax that required all people to buy salt rather than help themselves to the free salt lying on every beach, Gandhi had no answer. Instead of trying to respond immediately, he chose to be quiet and still for several days of prayer and reflection and listening. When he emerged from his self-imposed solitude, he announced that he would break the law by simply taking some ocean salt. To do this, he had to go to the ocean, so he began to walk across India. As he walked, people joined him, and news of his march spread around the world. Upon reaching the shore, he prayed, bathed in the water, and picked up a small portion of salt. Millions of people followed his example, and the British salt laws collapsed.[7]

A more recent example of the call to stillness before action came from James Forbes, pastor of Riverside Church in New York City, after the September 11 attacks on America. When asked on national television what our nation should do in response, he said, "Be still . . . be still . . . as a nation, as a people, we must be still." Forbes, an outspoken social activist and peacemaker, was not telling us to do nothing. He was calling us to prayer, to listening, to discernment. He was advising us to follow the same ancient wisdom posed in the form of two questions in the Chinese classic, the Tao Te Ching.

> Do you have the patience to wait
> till your mud settles and the water is clear?
> Can you remain unmoving
> till the right action arises by itself?[8]

Waiting patiently for the gift of discernment is not always possible. A job may need to be accepted or it will be given to someone else. The bus may be leaving for the demonstration at the Capitol and to participate you must be

EMBRACING THE WORLD

on it. A racial epithet may be directed at an old man at the shopping mall and you have only an instant to decide what to do. When time is of the essence, we are able to discern more quickly if we have been practicing the conditions that lead to discernment. Trusting in God, becoming still, living humbly, and opening ourselves to guidance will prepare us for those urgent experiences of discernment, for we will be living receptively with a readiness of heart and a listening soul.

Practicing Silence

Closely related to the quality of stillness is the practice of silence. Father Thomas Keating says that silence is the language of God and everything else is a poor translation. If this is true, then we must learn to be silent to hear God's love and mercy through the silence. Silence listening for silence? In our verbal world, this seems useless if not impossible. But think for a moment about listening to the wind. Do you actually hear the wind or do you hear the effects of the wind? You may hear leaves rustling, an unlatched gate banging, the neighbor's wind chime. When you listen, you hear the wind through the presence of tangible sources. When you listen to God in silence, you hear God and know God's presence through intangible sources such as the clarity of the intuition, the promptings of the heart, the creativity of the imagination, and the deep longings of the soul.

To listen in silence takes practice, for when we quiet the outer noises, the inner noises intensify. We must not try to banish the cacophony but rather pay attention to the inner voices and find our way through them, for listening to the inner noise is the path to silence. As you listen, you might ask yourself whether your inner voices are primarily memories coming from your past? Or are they plans or worries about the future? Do you tend to take an idea, a feeling, or a memory and enlarge it or escalate it through fantasy? Do you tend to discount or minimize your feelings or experience? We all have patterns in our inner noise. As we discover them, we do not judge them, for these patterns are neither good nor bad; they simply are. When we recognize and become familiar with them, we can greet them, let them go, and gently sink beneath them to the silence that awaits—the compassionate silence of God.

Outer silence can be practiced in small ways every day. You might turn off the car radio, forego the magazine as you wait in the doctor's office, walk around the block alone instead of going to the staff room at break time. As you practice outer silence, you will become more comfortable with the discipline of listening to your inner world and be able to welcome inner silence and find the delight and peace that awaits. The heart that knows silence can attune itself with God, receive guidance in subtle and unexpected ways, and discover the will of God.

The Will of God

A classic definition of *discernment* is "the art of finding God's will in the concrete life situations which confront us."[9] In our discussion thus far, I have been careful to avoid the term *God's will,* preferring instead the words *God's desire, God's yearning, God's guidance,* or *God's intent.* I have chosen these phrases because I have discovered over the years that when "God's will" is introduced, people get anxious, stuck on the concept, and unable to move to a more complete exploration of discernment. Because we have engaged in that exploration already, it is time to discover what God's will might mean to us.

During a retreat, I was exploring images for the "will of God" with the group gathered. For many people, the phrase evoked a linear image, such as an arrow, a straight road, or a measuring stick. Some told me that when God's will is imagined these ways, it feels absolute, exact, and sometimes punishing. "When I hear the term *the will of God,*" one woman said, "I feel like I am supposed to figure it out, stand up straight, and snap to!" "I feel like I am about to be judged and found lacking," a man added, "for how will I ever know the will of God?" These images lead us to what writer and spiritual director Rose Mary Dougherty calls "the feverish pursuit of God's will as though it were something outside us that we are left on our own to discover."[10]

When I suggested to the group a nonlinear image for the will of God such as a rainbow, or many winding roads headed in one general direction, or a sail boat that weaves its way to its destination, many participants began to relax and breathe more easily. Discernment was no longer a riddle to which God held the one right answer. Rather, discernment became a mutual endeavor in which God helps us find a new direction, encourages us in a next step, offers an open door when another closes behind us. These images seemed to be liberating, for they offer us the possibility of promise, of many options for faithfulness, and the idea that mistakes are part of the journey.

As we explored these images for the will of God and the place of mistakes in the discernment process, I read them the following story:

> After a long, hard climb up the mountain, the spiritual seekers finally found themselves in front of a great teacher. Bowing deeply, they asked the

question that had been burning inside them for so long: "How do we become wise?"

There was a long pause until the teacher emerged from meditation. Finally the reply came: "Good choices."

"But teacher, how do we make good choices?"

"From experience," responded the wise one.

"And how do we get experience?"

"Bad choices," smiled the teacher.[11]

Along with the freedom to make mistakes and learn from them as part of discernment, another liberating aspect of nonlinear images of God's will is freedom from the fear that God's will is in direct opposition to our personal will. Years ago, I remember thinking how awful it would be if, in the discernment of my path in justice and peace work, I discovered I was supposed to become a hospital worker, or sell everything and move to China, or become a gospel singer to proclaim the glory of the Lord. But when I thought about my fears, I realized that God would be very foolish to call me to places and actions for which I have no gifts. I faint at the sight of blood and have no aptitude for languages; and although I love to sing, I can never stay on key.

God's will honors our gifts and our life circumstance, offering options and possibilities and not just one way. God's will is *for* us, not against us. Remember the words of the prophet Jeremiah: "I know the plans I have for you, says the Lord, plans for your welfare and not for harm, to give you a future with hope" (Jeremiah 29:11). When we are hopeful and trust in a merciful God, we can wait for God's love to guide us. When we are faced with a life choice, we can ask of ourselves, with God as our witness, "What do I want? What do I really want?" and trust that through love an answer will be revealed.[12] As we stay focused on love, we may discover that God actually wants what we want and will bless us on our way.

Mistakes, uncertainty, ambiguity, and personal desires are all part of discerning the will of God. We can never know for certain the right course of action. God's will might never be absolutely clear. The most we can do is take a first hesitant step in a direction that feels right, then pause and ask ourselves if this movement is from love, with love, toward love. God's love for us and our love for God, for ourselves, our neighbors, and the world are at the heart of discernment. We could simply say that in praying for discernment we are asking to be guided by love—God's love and the love of and for others.

Discernment in Community

Although stillness and silence are important conditions for discernment, being still is not something we necessarily do alone with God. Other people can be very helpful by asking questions, offering options, and praying with us as we wait for answers. The Quaker tradition has long had a process for group discernment called the clearness committee.[13] Very simply, a person in the process of discernment gathers five or six trusted friends to hear the issue and then in an attitude of love and listening to ask questions. No problems are solved; advice is not given; opinions are not expressed. The clearness committee is a prayerful gathering and includes a natural rhythm of silence and speaking. There is no urgency and no expected outcome, only the hope that the process will help the person see and feel a little more clearly.

A story by Quaker activist and educator Parker Palmer can help us understand the process and the power a clearness committee can have in one's discernment.[14] When

Palmer was offered the position of president of a small educational institution, he was fairly certain he would take the job, but he gathered a clearness committee for the final discernment of his vocation. After the silent time at the beginning of the meeting, Palmer was asked a number of questions that he had already considered about the future of the institution and his place in it. Then out of the silence came a surprising question: "What would you like most about being president?" Parker began to answer with reasons he would not like to be president. After a few moments, his friend gently reminded him that he was asking what Parker would like. Palmer remembered his response: "I felt compelled to give the only honest answer I possessed, an answer that came from the very bottom of my barrel, an answer that appalled even me as I spoke it. 'Well,' said I, in the smallest voice I possess, 'I guess what I'd like most is getting my picture in the paper with the word president under it.'"[15]

The work and the love of the clearness committee led Palmer to understand that his desire to be president was ego-driven, not God-guided. His final answer revealed this truth. He realized that taking the job was not what he should do, for it would be bad for him and for the institution. With clarity and humility, Palmer was able to call the school and graciously refuse the position.

Another process for personal discernment in community is group spiritual direction. There are a number of variations on this process but, like the clearness committee, each method is prayerful and uses a rhythm of silence and speech that helps the person telling the story to listen well to the promptings of the spirit.[16] As one person struggles for clarity, other people's questions, reflections, suggestions, and experiences, offered in love, can help sort the voices of shoulds and oughts and ego from the true voice of love.

In one such setting, Louise, a member of the group, was struggling to decide whether she should make a year-long commitment to volunteer at a shelter for abused women and children. She had done some training and had volunteered sporadically, and now she had been invited to become part of the volunteer staff. She brought this issue of discernment to group spiritual direction. In this process, the presenter sits in a small circle with three or four group members who are willing to respond. They are surrounded by the other members of the group who listen and pray silently but offer no words.[17]

After the group members moved their chairs into the circular configuration, a verbal prayer was offered; they waited in silence until Louise was ready to speak. She began with the story of an old friend who had been emotionally battered in her marriage and how she was unable to leave because she had no place to go. This experience had drawn her to become involved with a shelter, but now she wondered if she should continue her work there. She was afraid she would feel helpless in the face of pain, be consumed by grief, or become overactive in the women's lives. She felt inadequate and guilty for what she called her "easy life." Her thoughts and feelings poured forth, and she did not attempt to be logical or clear; she simply spoke into the center of listening hearts.

When she was finished, the whole group honored three minutes of silence; then the responders offered their reflections one at a time. One person offered Louise a passage of scripture that, on reflection, might help her clarify the issues. Another said she had heard the gift of humility behind the fears and feelings of inadequacy. The third responder asked Louise to consider what she would do with her time if she did not accept the offer, and the fourth told her that as she listened she had received the image of a strongly rooted tree offering shelter to those who came to play, rest, or talk.

When each had spoken, they all entered another three minutes of silence, after which Louise thanked each of them and then quoted Mary, saying she would treasure their words and ponder them in her heart (Luke 2:19). The session ended with another minute of silence and an "Amen" from all.

In this process of group spiritual direction, the participants engage in no further discussion of any issue that has been brought to discernment, and no one except the presenter can bring up the topic again. This rule prevents anyone in the group from offering advice, trying to solve the problem, or pushing for a decision before it is time. It also ensures confidentiality and allows the discernment to continue after the group is over, as it did with Louise. She stayed in discernment in the days following the group by praying with the gifts she had received and allowing herself to not know. Weeks after the session, as she was folding laundry, Louise knew with a sense of clarity and peace that she would accept the position. She reported this to the group at their next meeting and said she was still afraid but was excited and hopeful and ready for the challenge ahead.

Clearness committees and group spiritual direction do not solve problems or give advice. Rather, they offer support and encouragement for deeper and deeper listening. This listening must be at the heart of our prayers for justice and peace, for we need to discover with God's help how we are to pray. Is my time best spent in intercessory prayer or in action? When I am called to action, where should I go to march, speak, or bear witness? Is it time for renewal, or is my longing to rest an avoidance of the suffering of the world? Am I being led to confession and forgiveness or into the apophatic way where God does the work of transformation in the secret of my soul? As we pray for discernment in the struggle for justice and peace, we are not choosing between good and bad; we are choosing among the many good possibilities that God offers to us. In fact, in praying for discernment we are not trying to choose simply a good life but rather we are trying to choose *our* life.[18] We are praying to discover the unique gift we each have to offer a world in pain.

An Invitation to Pray

Find a quiet place and take some time to reflect on ways God has guided you in the past. Then bring into your heart and mind a decision that you need to make that will affect the movement of your life and the lives around you. It may be as small as deciding how you will spend the weekend or as large as a change of career, a decision about your health, or an issue in relationship. See if you are willing to listen to God who loves you, and if you are, let go into the mystery of not knowing. Stay with your listening prayer as long as you can, then breathe a prayer of gratitude for the time you have spent with the Holy. Over the next weeks, develop a rhythm of thinking about your decision, gathering information, talking with people you trust, then letting go daily into a receptive time with God. You may not receive an answer of absolute clarity, but you will be practicing the art of discernment by listening for God's hope and will and promise in your life. Attuning your life with God's will connects you to all people who are willing to be guided so that God's promise of a just and peaceful world can be fulfilled.

CHAPTER SEVEN

TRUSTING THE
MERCY OF GOD

Mercy is God's innermost being turned outward to sustain the visible and created world in unbreakable love.
—CYNTHIA BOURGEAULT

In the spring of 1999, two students at Columbine High School in Littleton, Colorado, killed twelve classmates and one teacher before turning their guns on themselves. Many people were wounded; hundreds witnessed the carnage, and the whole community was traumatized. Some people tried to assign blame for the rampage with the desire to hold someone or something responsible. Others sought to discover causes, motivation, and warning signs so as to prevent future school killings. Still others turned their attention to healing and reconciliation and the possibility of new life. Many in these groups did not respect the positions of others, and harsh words and accusations flew back and forth. Everyone was hurting and desperately needed help.

One of the pastors in a large church not far from the high school told me how she and so many others in the religious community were called on to offer spiritual care to the traumatized. "I listened to their shock and their pain and tried to hold it in the context of a loving and merciful God," she said. "Even in the face of such tragedy, I do trust the mercy of God, but I cannot point it out to others; I have no easy words of comfort. All I could do was weep with them, as I believe God in His mercy weeps with all of us."

Another pastor shared how hard it was to preach in the weeks following the massacre. "I wanted to be pastoral and address the pain," he told me. "But I also felt the need to be prophetic and speak of the commitment to peace, even in the midst of violence and call everyone to compassion for perpetrators and their families as well as for the victims. But how could I preach the message of mercy and forgiveness to people raw with grief? How would I assure them of God's all-inclusive love?"

These two pastors articulate the confusion and the theological struggle that many of us face when confronted with violence, war, and tragedy. How could a loving and merciful God allow this to happen? Couldn't God have intervened to prevent the tragedy? If God saved some, why did God leave others to die? Where is God's power? Where is God's justice? Can we trust in the mercy of God when besieged with such questions? And what is the mercy of God?

Mercy with Mercy within Mercy

Thomas Merton's evocative name for God—mercy with mercy, mercy within mercy[1]—brings to mind relationship, connection, and bonds that are close and enfolding. This relational image of the mercy of God is validated by the original Semitic word *chesed* that is often translated in our Bibles as "mercy." *Chesed* actually means a fierce and committed love, a passionate relationship, an unbreakable connection.[2] Episcopal priest Cynthia Bourgeault invites us to think of mercy "as a bond, an infallible link of love that holds the created and uncreated realms together. The mercy of God does not come and go, granted to some and refused to others. Why? Because it is unconditional—always there, underlying everything. It is literally the force that holds everything in existence, the gravitational field in which we live and move and have our being."[3]

Trusting the mercy of God to be unconditional, always there, and underlying everything is easier when we experience healing, reconciliation, and justice. When a family lets go of old animosities, when people join together to fight crime and protect children, or when free elections are finally held in a war-torn country, we joyfully give thanks to a merciful God. But in times of continual violence and random tragedy, our trust in the mercy of God may get shaky or sometimes disappear altogether.

When I was a young adult traveling in Europe, I witnessed a man killed by a speeding taxi on a Paris street. I had recently left an ecumenical work camp in Holland, where twenty-four of us had lived together in a church, studied the Bible, prayed, worshipped, and helped build a community center for the neighborhood children. The mercy of God was palpable at the church, at the work site, throughout the community, and in the children's eyes. We were deeply connected and committed to each other and to God. However, the sight of instant, random death shattered my faith in the loving and merciful God I had discovered at camp, and when I returned to college I stopped attending church, forgot my devotions, and turned away from religion to study philosophy and psychology. I believed God had let me down.

Many years went by before I was able to reconcile the mercy of God I had experienced at camp with the tragedy and suffering I witnessed so shortly after. Through other life experiences, I realized that a merciful God does not keep us safe from harm but rather gives us a refuge and a haven—an unbreakable bond of love to cling to in the midst of our suffering. My faith was strengthened by these words in the book of Deuteronomy: "In your distress . . . you will return to the Lord your God and heed him. Because the Lord your God is a merciful God, he will neither abandon you or destroy you; he will not forget the covenant with your ancestors that he swore to them (Deuteronomy 4:30–31).

This passage was also a comfort to Anthony, an environmental activist working to preserve more land for future generations by having it designated as national wilderness area. "I get so discouraged by the greed and self-interest I witness," he said. "But I take seriously our responsibility to care for the land and all of God's creation. I believe that is part of God's covenant with us. It is important to trust that God will not forget this covenant and will not abandon us. When I don't see the mercy of God in front of me, I try to feel that mercy within my own heart, then live it and speak it for others to see."

Feeling the mercy of God in our own hearts and allowing God's mercy to guide our lives is one way we can trust the mercy of God in the midst of disappointment and tragedy. God may not seem to intervene in the events unfolding before us, but God is always at work in our hearts and the hearts of others, strengthening the bond of fierce and committed love. During times of tragedy, we often hear tales of ordinary people reaching out to those in need. Men and women at war sometimes remember a small kindness offered by the enemy. During interpersonal or institutional conflict, unlikely people may step forward to mediate and help bring about healing and reconciliation. When hearts and lives become merciful, we experience God's merciful intervention in the world.

For years, I have witnessed this merciful intervention through Toni Cook, pastor of St. Paul's United Methodist

Church in Denver, a small and financially struggling church in the inner city. Lack of money has not defeated the programs that she and the people of the congregation have envisioned, begun, and sustained. Over the past fourteen years, they have fed the homeless before church every Sunday. They initiated and now support a shelter for homeless youth, and they established a weekly dialogue between Buddhists and Christians that is followed by a joint meditation and prayer service. Although I have never asked the pastor if she experiences the mercy of God in her heart and in the hearts of those in her congregation, I find it hard to believe they could do all their loving service without that faith. When I am blessed to be part of that ministry, I find myself trusting more deeply in a God who passionately loves us all and who will not abandon us, even in our darkest hour.

Do you know someone who trusts in the mercy of God? Maybe a child who sings out to God, "Hello God! Here I am," knowing that God is waiting for and rejoices in that greeting. Maybe a friend who arrived to take you and your son out to dinner the night you lost your job. Maybe a gifted violinist who always makes time to encourage younger musicians, sharing his experiences and introducing them to others who can further their careers. Maybe an old woman who looks back on her difficult life without bitterness and says, "I have been blessed. In the midst of struggle I have never been alone." They may never have told you directly, but you recognize their faith in their words and actions and by the way they treat themselves and others. To find people who trust the mercy of God and to experience God's mercy in our own lives, we must wake up and pay attention to the present moment or we will miss the mercy that surrounds us.

Paying Attention to the Mercy of God

Have you ever had the startling experience of arriving home in your car but having no recollection of how you got there? You cannot remember the turns, the cars you passed, the color of the sky, or the sounds of the road. You were driving on automatic and not paying attention. You were somewhere else pursuing your fantasies, planning a meal, finishing an argument, counting your money, or worrying about your children. You were not awake to the present moment.

A Buddhist teaching tale recounts a disciple questioning the Zen master about the necessity of spiritual practice in his life.

> "Is there anything I can do to make myself enlightened?"
>
> "As little as you can do to make the sun rise in the morning."
>
> "Then of what use are the spiritual exercises you prescribe?"
>
> "To make sure you are not asleep when the sun begins to rise."[4]

We must not be asleep when the mercy of God shines on us and our world. We need to wake up and pay attention. As children, we learned from parents and teachers who were always telling us to pay attention. "Stop at the corner and look both ways!" a parent might say, or "Pay close attention when you are using those scissors." "Turn around and face front and pay attention to the lesson," teachers often say to wiggling children. "You'll get behind if you don't pay attention!" The adults in our lives were teaching us to pay attention to the outer world, to them, and to their instructions. They did this to keep us safe and to teach us what they believed to be important. And what they did was good, for we had to learn to pay attention if we were to navigate the world in safety.

However, staying awake spiritually is different from the lessons of attention we learned as children. As adults, we must now learn to pay attention to the inner world. We place our attention on the movement of the spirit in our hearts and in the hearts of others. We listen and attend to God's still, small voice. We stay awake and watch for the mercy of God. Staying awake and paying attention is hard work and takes practice. But the more we are able to do it, the more we will discover the miracle of living in the present and realize how each moment is filled with the grace and the mercy of God.

Instead of trying to think your way into these concepts of attention, you may wish to try the following exercise to experience the wonder of staying awake.

Begin by finding a comfortable place to sit. Settle yourself in the chair and allow your body to relax. Turn your attention to your breathing, simply following it in and out, in and out. Do not change your breathing pattern; simply attend to it. Allow your eyes to close and turn your attention to listening. What do you hear? Listen with all of who you are, not judging one sound as good and another as bad. Simply listen, taking all the time you need. Then gently ask yourself, "How do I hear the mercy of God?" If your mind wanders, gently bring it back to all you are hearing and ask yourself again, "How do I hear the mercy of God?" Continue to listen and ask, listen and ask as long as you wish. Then end your attentive time with a brief prayer of gratitude for what you heard and experienced. Bring your attention back to the room in which you are sitting, your body in the chair, your feet on the floor. When you are ready, open your eyes and reflect for a moment on how you experienced the mercy of God.

This brief practice can be done with your attention on any one of your senses, leading to the questions:

How do I see the mercy of God?
How do I touch the mercy of God?
How do I taste and smell the mercy of God?

Remember as you do this that we have defined *mercy* as "the infallible link of love that holds the created and uncreated realms together."[5]

As you practice attending to the mercy of God through your senses, you might begin to pay attention not only in meditation time but throughout your waking hours. You can look for the mercy of God in the way people treat each other, in a spring flower or a fall leaf, in the news of the escalation of war, in the taste of warm bread or cool water, in the sounds of sirens, in the feelings in your own heart. As you pay attention to the mercy of God that surrounds you, you will be guided to be merciful in your work and your prayers for justice and peace.

The making of peace depends on our willingness to see what is before us. The need to attend to the present moment (and the problems that occur when we do not) is addressed by Jesus in the gospel of Luke. Jesus was approaching Jerusalem on what we now call Palm Sunday. The crowds were welcoming him with shouts of blessing and praising God for all the deeds of power they had seen. Yet when Jesus saw his beloved city, he wept. "As he came near and saw the city, he wept over it, saying, 'If you, even you, had only recognized on this day the things that make for peace! But now they are hidden from your eyes'" (Luke 19:41–42).

Jesus' words call us to the present moment, to recognize the mercy of God, and to see the things that make for peace. Through daily practice, we can recognize the pervasiveness of God's mercy; our trust will grow, and we will find ourselves more ready and able to pray for justice and peace to a merciful God.

Praying to a Merciful God

The image of God we hold as we pray affects our experience of God, ourselves, others, and the world. When all our prayers for justice and peace are directed to and done in the name of a merciful God, we become a reflection of that mercy in the world. If I pray to a merciful God for economic justice for the people in Central America, I am reminded of my bond with them, my commitment to their welfare, and my connection to those who oppress. When I see no change for the people in poverty and feel great pain, I am comforted by God's mercy. I am also strengthened by the unbreakable bond of love with the people and with God to persevere in my prayers.

Praying to a merciful God makes it safe for us to cry out our anger and our desire for revenge as we discussed in Chapters Two and Five. If we pray our angry prayers while holding the image of a vengeful God, we are likely to become a reflection of that vengeance by acting on our frustrations and despair and taking personal revenge against another. Prayers to a God of vengeance perpetuate violence, harden our hearts, and keep us from seeking restorative justice, whereas prayers to a merciful God, even prayers that rage, soften our hearts and guide us toward hope.

Imagine how other images of God might affect our prayers. If our image of the Holy places God distant from and uninvolved in the created world, we are apt to pray without much hope of being heard. Our prayers then become abstract, and we may distance ourselves from the situation, denying any responsibility for bringing justice and peace to the world. If we believe in a God who is able to manipulate humankind and fix all our mistakes, we will be disappointed when our prayers are not answered with the solutions we have expected. Becoming a reflection of a manipulative God, we are also in danger of trying to fix and manipulate people and institutions that are not of our liking rather than trust the mercy of God to bring eventual healing and reconciliation.

In spoken and written prayers, how we address God will also influence our petitions, intercessions, and praise. Praying "God, ruler of the universe" will surely bring requests that are different than when we pray "God, mender of broken hearts." In your own prayers for justice and peace, try naming God in different ways and see how your prayers change. You might begin with "God who promises peace to our world." Then offer a prayer to "God of justice and might." Try "God of the sparrow," "Creator of life," "God who weeps with us," "Protector of the poor," or "Merciful God."

If some of these names for God do not match your experience of God, let them go and create other names for God that fit for you. Notice how your prayers change with different names and how some "God images" pull forth prayers you did not realize resided in your heart. Your prayers may be short, "arrow" prayers, designed to fly directly to the heart of God, or longer prayers in which you pour out your desires and longings, your pain and your joy. One of my favorite prayers for justice and peace is written by liturgist and writer Miriam Therese Winter and is addressed to a God of mercy and liberation:

> Look upon me, have mercy upon me, O Source of my liberation, for I am heavily burdened. The cares I carry are weighing me down. I am losing all perspective. My eyes no longer see the stars in this never ending night. I am crippled by fear and anxiety when I think of the world we are handing on to succeeding generations. Bend down to me and lift me up to face myself with courage, to look the demonic straight in the eye and resist it with a song. Let me see to another's sorrow, share another's injustice, bear another's burdens, and in the process, lose my own. Teach me to care and not to care, bid my fear be still, and let all my insecurity lose itself in Your will. Amen.[6]

Praying for others and the world, praying for renewal, transformation, or discernment to a loving, merciful, liberating God in words, silence, or action brings us hope. Even in her acknowledgment of darkness, fear, and anxiety, Winter's prayer rings with hope. She affirms that we can find courage, that there is a way to resist lovingly, that we do share each other's burdens, that paradox is embraced, and that God's will will triumph. Trusting in the mercy of God and offering prayers to a merciful God keeps hope alive in our hearts and in the world.

Hoping Isn't Wishing

In my own life, I spend much time with the language of wishing circling my mind. "I wish it would rain," I think in the midst of a drought. "I wish they would listen to each other," I say as I read about the negotiations in the Middle East. "I wish that Congress would stop arguing," I complain as one more bill gets stalled.

Sometimes my wishing turns to the language of hope. "I hope they don't find cancer in the exploratory surgery." "I hope our new pastor will stay a long time." "I hope the medical relief reaches the refugees before winter." "I hope the demonstration is peaceful." I may exchange the words of wishing for hoping, but the shift does not bring me to the experience of sacred hope as long as I cling to my own desired outcome.

Sacred hope is open-ended, not attached to outcome; hope is patient and willing to wait. But this waiting is not passive, for it is alive with expectation and ready to receive whatever a merciful God has to offer. In the words of Roman Catholic priest and writer Henri Nouwen, sacred hope is born from the spiritual life "in which we wait, actively present to the moment, trusting that new things will happen . . . new things that are far beyond our own imagination, fantasy, or prediction."[7]

Another way to describe sacred hope is to understand that it is more of a perspective than an emotion. We can experience the emotions of sadness, anger, or despair and still be hopeful. We can feel the suffering of others or witness violence and still remain hopeful. When we hope, we recognize the tragedies of the present moment and at the same time are able to see beyond them. "Hope," according to Vaclav Havel, human rights advocate and the first president of the Czech Republic, "is a dimension of the soul, an orientation of the spirit."[8]

My friend Daniel fits Havel's definition of a hopeful man. He works with a ministry in the heart of the Tenderloin district in San Francisco, serving those who are homeless, impoverished, and chronically mentally ill. He loves his work, his colleagues, and the people he serves whom he calls "the people of the street who minister to me." He tells stories of how members of his Bible study groups have opened up the scriptures to him. "When you have been to hell and back, you find hidden meaning that scholars seem to miss," he says. Daniel does not wish for answers to the multiple problems he encounters; he does not wish to fix the systems or the people. With hope he engages individuals and groups, speaks out against systemic injustice, and encourages the life and dignity in each person he sees. He gets angry and frustrated and grieves the loss of potential in so many wounded people, but he returns to work each day filled with hope. Daniel's spirit is not defeated, and his soul is grounded in God.

Do you have hopeful people in your life? People who are able to wait expectantly, trusting that new things will happen, who do not hold on to their own wishes for the future? Hopeful people are a blessing to us, to others, and to the world. They are not always happy; they hurt with others who are hurting; they see clearly the problems that exist. But they are not defeated. Hope allows them to see beyond the present moment to a new and better day. They are not sure what that day will look like, what it will bring, or even what their own role will be. They know how important it is to stay fully present in the moment at the same time they face the future with hope. Trusting in the mercy of God, they know that all will be well.

All Shall Be Well

"All shall be well, and all shall be well, and all manner of thing shall be well,"[9] are words written by Julian of Norwich, a fourteenth-century English mystic who received a series of visions of Jesus crucified during one night when she was thirty years old. She wrote of her experience in the book *Revelations of Divine Love* in which these often-repeated words are found. During a class, I played a recording[10] of a choir singing these words over and over and asked the students to add their own voices to the refrain. After the meditation, a student responded not with hope but with disgust. "I cannot stand to sing those words," she said. "All is *not* well. Things are a mess in my life and the world. The words are a lie."

To believe the sacred hope in Julian's words, we need to recognize that she was proclaiming the future and not the present. And if we read her words, we see that her proclamation was written after her clear acknowledgment of sin. Julian struggled with sin and why God allowed it, but she remembered her vision in which Jesus said to her that sin was necessary. She explained Jesus' words by writing, "In the simple word sin our Lord reminded me in a general sort of way of all that is not good . . . of all the suffering and pain of . . . creation."[11] Mother Julian (as she came to be known) was not in denial about the ways of the world. She knew of illness, anguish, and death, but her trust in a merciful God revealed to her that all would be well.

Hopeful people who trust in the mercy of God remind us that we too can attend to merciful moments in our own lives, practice staying awake to the wonders that surround us, and wait expectantly on God. And while we trust and hope and wait, we pray and work for justice and peace. For we are active participants in the creation of the peaceful world that has been promised. Trust does not keep us from discernment. Patience does not teach us passivity. Hope does not rob us of the present moment. Rather, trusting, hoping, and waiting we pray passionately and embrace the world with the love and mercy we have received from God. With our prayers for justice and peace, we open our hearts and our arms to our sisters and brothers and all of creation. We are God's hope. God depends on us. Let us respond from hearts overflowing with love.

Spring has returned to the Rockies, and three years have passed since I began designing a class titled "Praying for Justice and Peace." In the months since I began writing *Embracing the World*, terrorists have attacked the United States, bombs have rained on Afghanistan, and the Middle East conflict between Israel and Palestine has escalated. The world situation intensified and deepened my writing process, and my earlier desire to write this book became a need. I believe writing has been my way of responding to the horror, grief, and fear I experience in the face of such violence. My hope is that reading this book has helped you find more courage to embrace our hurting world with prayers for justice and peace. How you pray is not so important; that you do pray is imperative. Pray alone, with your family, or in community. Whisper your prayers, recite your prayers, march your prayers, shout your prayers. Sing, draw, dance your prayers. Pray as your heart leads you. Persevere in your prayers, trust in your prayers, and have faith in a God who hears your prayers. In this time of trial, how can we do less?

Denver, Colorado
Eastertide 2002

Preface

1. Thanks to Laura Folkwein for this description of herself.
2. Jim Forest, "Thomas Merton: A Friend Remembered." In *Peace Is the Way: Writings on Nonviolence from the Fellowship of Reconciliation*, Walter Wink, ed. (New York: Orbis Books, 2000), 92.

Chapter One

Epigraph: Edwina Gateley, Keynote Address, Ecumenical Women's Conference, August 18, 2001, Denver, Colorado.

1. Dorothy Friesen, "Social Action and the Need for Prayer." In *Peace Is the Way: Writings on Nonviolence from the Fellowship of Reconciliation*, Walter Wink, ed. (New York: Orbis Books, 2000), 124.
2. Dorothee Soelle, *The Silent Cry: Mysticism and Resistance* (Minneapolis: Augsburg Fortress Press, 2001), 201.
3. Quoted in *Spirit Unfolding: The Newsletter of the Spiritual Development Network of the United Church of Christ.* Marjorie Colton, ed., Winter 1997, p. 1.
4. Marcus Borg, *Reading the Bible Again for the First Time* (San Francisco: HarperSanFrancisco, 2001), 139.
5. Ibid., p. 139.
6. William Shakespeare, *The Merchant of Venice*, Act 4, Scene 1, lines 181–184.
7. Gerald Sittser, "The Life and Death We Don't Deserve." *The Christian Century* (Chicago: Christian Century Foundation, 1996), 44–47.
8. Ibid., p. 45.
9. Ibid., p. 46.
10. Ibid., p. 47.
11. Shakespeare, lines 192–194.
12. Desmond Mpilo Tutu, *No Future Without Forgiveness* (New York: Doubleday, 1999), 54–55.

13. I discuss this topic in depth in *Praying with Body and Soul* (Minneapolis: Augsburg Fortress, 1998), 109–112.
14. Walter Brueggemann, *Peace* (St. Louis: Chalice Press, 2001), 15.
15. Danny A. Belrose, Keynote Address, 2001 Peace Colloquy, November 4, 2001, Independence, Missouri.
16. Brueggemann, pp. 2–3.
17. Ibid., p. 5.

Chapter Two

Epigraph: Walter Wink, *The Powers That Be: Theology for a New Millennium* (New York: Doubleday, 1989), 185.

1. Anne Kleinkopf, unpublished paper, Iliff School of Theology, Fall 2001.
2. Betty Brown, unpublished paper, Iliff School of Theology, Fall 2001.
3. Dorothy Friesen, "Social Action and the Need for Prayer." In *Peace Is the Way: Writings on Nonviolence from the Fellowship of Reconciliation*, Walter Wink, ed. (New York: Orbis Books, 2000), 124.
4. Ibid., p. 125.
5. Quoted in Jack Kornfield, *After the Ecstasy the Laundry* (New York: Bantam Books, 2000), 74.
6. *Cowley*, a pamphlet published by the Society of St. John the Evangelist, Winter 2002, *27*(3), 3.
7. Thich Nhat Hanh, *Being Peace* (Berkeley, Calif.: Parallax Press, 1987), 80.
8. Neil Douglas-Klotz, *Prayers of the Cosmos* (San Francisco: HarperSanFrancisco, 1990), 85.
9. A. Manette Ansay, *Limbo* (New York: HarperCollins, 2001), 74–75.
10. Elias Chacour, *Blood Brothers* (Grand Rapids, Mich.: Baker Book House Company, 1984), 62.
11. Ibid., p. 49.
12. William F. May, "Liturgy for Life." *The Christian Century*, 2001, *181*(24), 28.

13. Joseph Nassal, *Premeditated Mercy* (Leavenworth, Kans.: Forest of Peace Publishing, 2000), 137.
14. Quoted in Richard J. Foster, *Prayer: Finding the Heart's True Home* (New York: HarperCollins, 1992), 197.
15. Ibid., p. 197.
16. Ibid., p. 247.
17. Wink, p. 93.
18. Ibid., p. 31.
19. Ibid., p. 192.
20. Ibid., p. 33.
21. Ibid., p. 195.
22. Douglas V. Steere, "Intercession: Caring for Souls." *Weavings: A Journal of the Christian Spiritual Life,* March/April, 1989, 4(2), 19.
23. Wink, p. 185.
24. Foster, p. 249.

Chapter Three

Epigraph: Quoted in Roger Walsh, *Essential Spirituality: The 7 Central Practices to Awaken Heart and Mind* (New York: Wiley, 1999), 271.
1. Carol Rittner and Sondra Myers, eds., *The Courage to Care* (New York: New York University Press, 1986), 99.
2. Walsh, p. 263.
3. Jim Douglas, "The Nuclear Train Campaign." In *The Rise of Christian Conscience,* Jim Wallis, ed. (San Francisco: Harper-SanFrancisco, 1987), 64.
4. Kate Stevens, "UCC Pastor Called to Bear Witness in D.C." *Cleveland: United Church News,* July/August, 2001, p. A8.
5. Ibid., p. A8.
6. Ibid.
7. Richard K. Taylor, "With All Due Respect: A Historical Perspective on Civil Disobedience." In *The Rise of Christian Conscience,* Jim Wallis, ed. (San Francisco: HarperSanFrancisco, 1987), 250.
8. Ibid., p. 252.

9. Ibid.

10. Jim Douglas, "Civil Disobedience as Prayer." In *Peace Is the Way: Writings on Nonviolence from the Fellowship of Reconciliation,* Walter Wink, ed. (New York: Orbis Books, 2000), 149.

11. *I Am the Way: Constitution of the Sisters of Loretto at the Foot of the Cross* (Nerinx, Ky.: Sisters of Loretto, 1997), 13.

12. Douglas, "Civil Disobedience as Prayer," p. 150.

13. Andrew Young, *An Easy Burden* (New York: HarperCollins, 1996), 178.

14. Bernie Glassman, *Bearing Witness* (New York: Crown Publishers, 1998).

15. Michelle Negron Bueno, "Why Am I Here?" *The Other Side,* January/February, 2002, 1–2.

16. Renee Dreiling, Dominican Sisters of Great Bend, Kans., private correspondence, 1995–2001.

17. Walsh, p. 265.

18. Jim Forest, "Thomas Merton, A Friend Remembered." In *Peace Is the Way: Writings on Nonviolence from the Fellowship of Reconciliation,* Walter Wink, ed. (New York: Orbis Books, 2000), 91–92.

19. Richard Rohr, *Everything Belongs: The Gift of Contemplative Prayer* (New York: The Crossroad Publishing Company, 1999), 144.

Chapter Four

Epigraph: Wayne Muller, *Sabbath: Restoring the Sacred Rhythm of Rest* (New York: Bantam Books, 1999), 159.

1. Inspired by a story told by Edwina Gateley at the Ecumenical Women's Conference, August 18, 2001, Denver, Colorado.

2. Thomas Merton, *Conjectures of a Guilty Bystander* (Garden City, N.Y.: Image Books, 1968), 86.

3. Parker Palmer, "Leading from Within." In *Spirit at Work: Discovering the Spirituality in Leadership* (San Francisco: Jossey-Bass, 1994), 35.

4. Oscar Romero, "Prophets of a Future Not Our Own," http://wagingpeace.org/hero/oscar_romero.html.

5. Dorothee Soelle, *The Silent Cry: Mysticism and Resistance* (Minneapolis: Augsburg Fortress Press, 2001), 206.

6. Rose Barber, unpublished paper, Iliff School of Theology, Fall 2001.

7. Stella Mae Schlegel, unpublished paper, Iliff School of Theology, Fall 2001.

8. Soelle, p. 202.

9. Laura Folkwein, unpublished paper, Iliff School of Theology, Fall 2001.

10. Sally Rogers, "Love Will Guide Us." In *Singing the Living Tradition* (Boston: Unitarian Universalist Association, 1993), 131.

11. Si Kahn, "People Like You." Joe Hill Music, MCS Music America, Inc., Nashville, 1981.

12. Soelle, p. 252.

13. Muller, p. 162.

14. St. Bernard Clairvaux, *On the Song of Songs.* Quoted in *Great Devotional Classics: Selections from the Writings of Bernard of Clairvaux,* Douglas Steere, ed. (Nashville, Tenn.: The Upper Room, 1961), 24.

15. Edward Hays, *Pray All Ways* (Easton, Kans.: Forest of Peace Books, 1981), 157.

Chapter Five

Epigraph: Quoted in *Spirit Unfolding: The Newsletter of the Spiritual Development Network of the United Church of Christ.* Marjorie Colton, ed., Winter 1997, 1.

1. Deborah Sanchez, unpublished paper, Iliff School of Theology, Fall 2001.

2. Harriet Mullaney, unpublished paper, Iliff School of Theology, Fall 2001.

3. Attributed to Mahatma Gandhi.

4. "What Does God Intend?" *The Christian Century,* 2001, *118*(26), 3.

5. Susan Kling, "Baptism by Fire: The Story of Fannie Lou Hamer." In *The Universe Bends Toward Justice,* Angie O'Gorman, ed. (Philadelphia: New Society Publishers, 1990), 153.

6. Marie Marchand, unpublished paper, Iliff School of Theology, Fall 2001.

7. Desmond Mpilo Tutu, *No Future Without Forgiveness* (New York: Doubleday, 1999), 156.

8. Matthew Fox, *Meditations with Meister Eckhart* (Santa Fe, N.Mex.: 1983), 52.

9. See, for example, Thomas Keating, *Open Mind, Open Heart: The Contemplative Dimension of the Gospel* (Amity, N.Y.: Amity House, 1986).

10. Dorothee Soelle, *The Silent Cry: Mysticism and Resistance* (Minneapolis: Augsburg Fortress Press, 2001), Chapter 15.

11. Quoted in Jed McKenna, *Spiritual Enlightenment: The Damnedest Thing* (Fairfield, Iowa: Wisefool Press, 2002), 20.

Chapter Six

Epigraph: Patricia Loring, *Spiritual Discernment: The Context and Goal of Clearness Committees* (Wallingford, Penn.: Pendle Hill Publications, 1992), 24.

1. Susan G. Farnham, Joseph P. Gill, R. Taylor McLean, and Susan M. Ward, *Listening Hearts: Discerning Call in Community* (Harrisburg, Penn.: Morehouse, 2000), 26.

2. Paul Wilkes, *Beyond the Walls: Monastic Wisdom for Everyday Life* (New York: Doubleday, 1999), 121.

3. Wendy Wright, "Passing Angels: The Arts of Spiritual Direction." *Weavings: A Journal of the Christian Spiritual Life,* November/December 1985, *10*(6), 12.

4. Jennifer Cook, unpublished paper, Iliff School of Theology, Fall 2001.

5. This insight was shared by Marjory J. Thompson during an address at the Spiritual Leaders Conference: A Gathering for Discernment, August 14, 2001, Syracuse, Indiana.

6. Farnham, p. 33.
7. Roger Walsh, *Essential Spirituality: The 7 Central Practices to Awaken Heart and Mind* (New York: Wiley, 1999), 276.
8. Wayne Muller, *Sabbath: Restoring the Sacred Rhythm of Rest* (New York: Bantam Books, 1999), 169.
9. Thomas H. Green, *Weeds Among the Wheat, Discernment: Where Prayer and Action Meet* (Notre Dame, Ind.: Ave Maria Press, 2000), 57.
10. Rose Mary Dougherty, *Group Spiritual Direction: Community for Discernment* (Mahwah, N.J.: Paulist Press, 1995), 31.
11. Walsh, p. 239.
12. Dougherty, p. 31.
13. Loring, pp. 3–26.
14. Parker J. Palmer, *Let Your Life Speak: Listening for the Voice of Vocation* (San Francisco: Jossey-Bass, 2000), 44–47.
15. Ibid., p. 46.
16. For a full discussion of the practice of group spiritual direction, see Rose Mary Dougherty, *Group Spiritual Direction: Community for Discernment* (Mahwah, N.J.: Paulist Press, 1995).
17. I explore this method of group spiritual direction in *Be Still: Designing and Leading Contemplative Retreats* (Bethesda, Md.: Alban Institute, 2000), 76–80.
18. Flora Wuellner, "Were Not Our Hearts Burning Within Us?" *Weavings: A Journal of the Christian Spiritual Life*, November/December 1985, *10*(6), 33.

Chapter Seven

Epigraph: Cynthia Bourgeault, *Mystical Hope: Trusting in the Mercy of God* (Boston: Cowley Publications, 2001), 25.
1. Jim Forest, "Thomas Merton, A Friend Remembered." In *Peace Is the Way: Writings on Nonviolence from the Fellowship of Reconciliation*, Walter Wink, ed. (New York: Orbis Books, 2000), 92.
2. Bourgeault, p. 4.

3. Ibid., p. 25.
4. Quoted in Richard Rohr, *Everything Belongs: The Gift of Contemplative Prayer* (New York: Crossroad, 1999), 53.
5. Bourgault, p. 25.
6. Miriam Therese Winter, "Look upon me, have mercy upon me. . . . " In *Soul Weavings: A Gathering of Women's Prayers*, Lyn Klug, ed. (Minneapolis: Augsburg Fortress, 1996), 119.
7. Henri J. M. Nouwen, "A Spirituality of Waiting." *Weavings: A Journal of the Christian Spiritual Life*, John S. Mogabgab, ed., January/February 1987, 2(1), 11.
8. Quoted in a Christmas letter from a friend.
9. Julian of Norwich, *Revelations of Divine Love*, Clifton Wolters, trans. (London: Penguin Books, 1966), 35 and 103.
10. Steven C. Warner, "All Will Be Well." In *The Seven Signs: Music to Celebrate the Sacraments* (Schiller Park, Ill.: World Library Publications, 1999), 15.
11. Julian of Norwich, p. 103.

Glassman, Bernie. *Bearing Witness*. New York: Crown Publishers, 1998.

Hanh, Thich Nhat. *Being Peace*. Berkeley, Calif.: Parallax Press, 1987.

Hollyday, Joyce. *Then Shall Your Light Rise: Spiritual Formation and Social Witness*. Nashville, Tenn.: Upper Rooms Books, 1997.

Lederach, John P. *Building Peace: Sustainable Reconciliation in Divided Societies*. Washington, D.C.: U.S. Institute for Peace, 1997.

Lusseyran, Jacques. *And There Was Light: Autobiography of Jacques Lusseyran*. New York: Parabola Books, 1963.

Muller, Wayne. *Sabbath: Restoring the Sacred Rhythm of Rest*. New York: Bantam Books, 1999.

Nassal, Joseph. *Premeditated Mercy*. Leavenworth, Kans.: Forest of Peace Publishing, 2000.

Nouwen, Henri. *The Road to Peace*. New York: Orbis Books, 1998.

Soelle, Dorothee. *The Silent Cry: Mysticism and Resistance*. Minneapolis: Augsburg Fortress Press, 2001.

Tutu, Desmond Mpilo. *No Future Without Forgiveness*. New York: Doubleday, 1999.

Wink, Walter, ed. *Peace Is the Way: Writings on Nonviolence from the Fellowship of Reconciliation*. New York: Orbis Books, 2000.

Wink, Walter. *The Powers That Be: Theology for a New Millennium*. New York: Doubleday, 1989.

ACKNOWLEDGMENTS

A friend of mine who writes books on spirituality and family life said that she could not imagine lecturing or teaching something she had not written. I told her that my experience was just the opposite; I could not imagine writing something I had not already taught. Teaching is my most fundamental call in life, and everything I have written flows from the experience. Over many years of teaching, I have realized that I teach best what I am trying to learn, and my writing continues that learning process.

Therefore, I wish to honor those who have helped me learn—the students and retreatants whose questions, challenges, ideas, stories, and prayers grace these pages. Many of you are named in the text, others in the notes; some of you are disguised, and a number of you will believe I used nothing of your individual wisdom. But discussions in which you may have been vocal or silent are an integral part of my creative process, so even if you cannot find yourself in the words of this book, know that you are present.

Others who helped me learn were those I interviewed about their work and prayers for peace and justice: Carter Case, Lucia Guzman, Gretchen Hawley, Cecily Jones, Krysso Heart LeFey, Judith Nelson and Carol White, Sala Nolan, Anne Sayre, Betty and Dale Schwicker, Gail Eisman Valeta, and Patrick Welage. I am most grateful for your time, experiences, and encouragement.

During my teaching and writing, a number of people asked me evocative questions, handed me books, or told me stories that jogged my thinking, added a missing piece, or helped me go into realms I had not considered. You may not have any idea of your contribution but it was invaluable. Thank you Lee Ann Bryce, Ginny Chase, Kathy Coffey, Michelle Danson, Carol Fox, Elise Guest, Jerry Haas, Malcom Himshoot, Glen Hinson, Barbara Hulac, Margaret Johnson, Daniel O'Connor, Pat Schaffer, Bob Simpson, Nora Smith, Karen Stoffers, Marjory Thompson, Ruth Warren, and Lisa Womak.

Turning the full oral experience of teaching—lecture notes, memories of discussions, prayers offered, and stories shared—into written form and ultimately into a book depends on the wisdom and guidance of many experts. Sheryl Fullerton, my editor, heard this book within the stories I told with her over lunch. She shepherded it through the proposal process, and when I began to write she gave me encouragement as well as suggestions and criticism. After reworking one section for the fifth time, I called to tell her she was "one tough editor." To me that is a supreme compliment, for Sheryl did not allow anything to slip by her commitment to clarity or her desire for words and stories to touch the reader's heart.

Once a manuscript is finished, it is released to other competent people who edit, design, produce, and market it, creating the book you hold in your hands today. The team at Jossey-Bass who accomplished this task includes Chandrika Madhavan, Mark Kerr, Jessica Egbert, Erin Jow, Andrea Flint, and copyeditor Mary O'Briant. I met the team early in the writing process and was excited by their interest in the book and their dedication to the creative process. For all your work behind the scenes and your attention to detail, I give thanks.

In addition to the team at Jossey-Bass, I was assisted by two other dedicated women. My patient and efficient secretary Cathie Woehl typed and retyped the manuscript, never complaining about the many times I changed my mind about a phrase, a word, or the order of the paragraphs. Debbie Hunter, my student assistant, searched the Internet for references, spent hours in the library seeking books I needed, and put all my endnotes into proper form. She was a calm presence in the midst of a sometimes chaotic process.

Presenting the material as I write, think, and pray grounds me in the world about which I write and helps keep me from simplistic abstractions and disembodied ideas. A number of places invited and welcomed my work in progress. Thank you to those who asked me to participate in the Vancouver School of Theology faculty lecture series; the Spiritual Directors International Conference in Atchinson, Kansas; the Presbytery of Pueblo, Colorado; the Woman's Story Retreat at Mount Saint Francis Center in Colorado Springs, Colorado; the Peace Colloquy 2001 in Independence, Missouri; the "Lunch with a Professor" lecture series at the Iliff School of Theology, and Sixth Avenue United Church of Christ, my home church in Denver, Colorado.

The Sacred Heart Jesuit Retreat House in Sedalia, Colorado, welcomed me into one of their hermitages, where I was able to write free from distractions, participate in community worship, be held in prayer, and receive an unending supply of cookies. Thank you Fr. Lou McCabe and the retreat house staff for your hospitality.

Trish Dunn, Joan Erickson, Beth Gaede, Holly Heuer, Margaret Johnson, Sharyl Peterson, Margie Tyler, and Kay Young read sections along the way and offered suggestions, corrections, and encouragement. Every writer should be blessed with such honest, perceptive readers.

And finally, I thank my husband, Jim Laurie. There are no words to express the depth of my gratitude.

THE AUTHOR

Jane E. Vennard is ordained to a special ministry of teaching and spiritual direction in the United Church of Christ. She is senior adjunct faculty of prayer and spirituality at the Iliff School of Theology in Denver. In addition, Jane is a spiritual director in private practice, teaches classes in a variety of ecumenical settings, and leads retreats nationally. She is the author of numerous articles, as well as three other books: *Praying for Friends and Enemies, Praying with Body and Soul,* and *Be Still: Designing and Leading Contemplative Retreats.*

INDEX

aphatic, 81; to merciful God, 116–118; need for daily, 54–57; personal forms of, 61–62; for renewal, 52–68, 71–72; of supplication, 29–30; for transformation, 69–87

Prayer word, 83–85

Psalm 25:9, 96

Psalm 58:6-8, 76

Psalm 137, 25–26